An American Woman's
Zest for Living

by
Donna B. Dilsaver

This book is dedicated to my grandchildren, Katie, Kristen, and Danny Ryan, and Laura Parkhurst.

ACKNOWLEDGMENTS

This project would not have begun without the insistence of Eleanor Mayne nor the encouragement of Vice Admiral Kent Carroll. Most of life would not have been lived with zest without the love and support of my husband, Dick Dilsaver, or my son, Dr. Ron Ryan, and family.

Carreen Simon and her computer skills, Shannon Dannelley Littlejohn and her sharp editing pencil added to the professional result. Those who have participated also include Delores Oard, Faye Mohrbacher, Joyce Riggs Church, Beverly Hoover, my brother Kenneth, Jane Anderson, Marge Setter, Carl Williams, Holly Anderson and many other friends.

Special inspiration came from Dr. Elliot Engel of Raleigh, North Carolina, author, lecturer and professor.

All with God's grace.

An American Woman's Zest for Living

Copyright © 2008 by D. B. Dilsaver Publishing, Wichita
KS, 67026

This publication may not be reproduced, stored in a
retrieval system, or transmitted in whole or in part, in any
form by any means, electronic, mechanical, photocopying,
recording, or otherwise without prior permission of the
copyright holder.

International Standard Book Number: 978-0-615-26339-7

Library of Congress Control Number: 2008911383

Printed in the U.S.A by Mennonite Press, Inc., Newton,
Kansas

PROLOGUE

As democracy diminishes and individual freedoms decline in this country, those of us who lived in the 20th century have a tendency to think we were blessed with history's privilege of opportunities. It is for those privileges and blessings we voice our gratitude.

It was after retirement and into the years of mentoring young professionals, caregiving and serving on community boards, that a longtime friend repeatedly insisted I record my professional life.

I began organizing a file of notes, records and photos. They stayed in the files.

I was reluctant to publish my career history for I wanted no one to perceive my work to be a "vanity book." It would be a record of my career and an encouragement for those beginning to embrace challenges with pleasure. By example of accepting opportunities, I hope I have held true to that goal.

When I was living alone, one of Dick's friends encouraged me to do as he was doing, put my files into a book for my grandchildren. He wrote, "you have had a career most women can only dream about."

My thoughts came together in appreciation of the gift of being born at a time and in a country where women are free to pursue a professional career and contribute to the improvement of the human condition in the home, community, country and global endeavors.

Lessons learned in my youth through the Depression and World War II were invaluable to me as an adult.

For example, a day of celebration on the farm came after WWII when Kansas Gas and Electric Company built a half-mile electric line to the farmstead and turned "on" the electricity. Our lives changed.

Reliable power ran electric motors, lighting, refrigeration, cooling, milking machines and radio night and day

– all enhanced our lives and income.

On that day I was unaware that we were part of the most scientific and engineering feat of our century – the electrification of America. Modern accomplishments have been based on that not-so-simple transportation and distribution system of flipping a switch.

Nor on that spring day in 1947 did I give a thought to a career that would be a part of that successful task. Twenty years later I became a member of the communication staff of that electric utility, Kansas Gas and Electric Company. First promoting "Live Better Electrically," working on Kansas' first nuclear energy power plant, Wolf Creek Generating Station, and creating and implementing a nationally recognized energy education program.

During the individual and collective inventive, efficient and effective plural efforts we developed an unparalleled energy based economy in this nation. The only possible match might be the invention of the wheel, lever and cog developed over centuries.

Acknowledging that reality gave momentum to entering the 21st century with an information industry.

This condition includes removing the glass ceilings for women. A word of caution, when glass is shattered, even the minute pieces can inflict pain and permanent scars.

When the glass is slid aside like a pocket door to make an opening for gracious entry with respect for talent, value and intellect, it is a benefit to all who participate.

I have experienced both. The latter is far more rewarding.

Reflecting on my participation has been enlightening and rewarding as I acknowledge my many blessings and the support from all those who walked the walk with me.

My hopes for your future, my beloved grandchildren, is that you experience life abundantly and with a self-discovered zest for living.

Contents

1 The Gift of an Angel — **1**

2 Kansas and Me Under the Rainbow — **23**

3 Counting Boeing Bombers — **41**

4 Rapid-fire Lessons — **65**

5 Love, Loss and Life — **83**

6 A New Career – Electrically — **101**

7 Involve, Initiate, Improve — **111**

8 Women's Voice in Energy – a Nuclear Challenge — **135**

9 Retiring Midst a Beauty Pageant — **144**

10 New Directions — **184**

11 Care Giving, a Rewarding Choice — **216**

12 Adjustment, with Support from Family and Friends — **221**

Celebrating a Zest for Living — **238**

On behalf of The Executive Board and all members of Women in Energy, we wish to express our sincere appreciation to:

DONNA DILSAVER

You have provided distinguished service as founder and Executive Board Chairman of WOMEN IN ENERGY.

You have demonstrated exceptional dedication and perseverance in pioneering and establishing the organization to encourage, foster, stimulate and promote research, knowledge and understanding about all forms of energy.

You have given freely of your time and effort, professionally and personally, by providing outstanding leadership in accomplishing the organization's objectives.

You have provided encouragement in developing the knowledge and skills of Women in Energy, recognizing the value in the fulfillment of human potential.

For this and more, we extend to you our deepest gratitude.

Presented March 24, 1981

1. The Gift of an Angel

I was born free and independent. I was not to be segregated. I was not to be subjugated. Beginning with Henry Sampson who came on the Mayflower and all who came thereafter, my family helped build for me a country based on democratic and religious principals to assure me of these freedoms. My life has been lived with these assumptions and these protections, even though I entered this world at a difficult time for our country.

It must have been a depressing day for Juanita as she lay in the same bedroom in the farm house where she was born 25 years earlier, near Oatville, Kansas.

That Tuesday, the 19th day of July, one of the hottest days on record and in mid-afternoon, into the seventh hour of labor, she finally delivered a 7-pound 2-ounce baby girl. Her mother was her mid-wife. The doctor arrived two hours later at the same time her husband came home from work.

I was the third child born to Raymond and Juanita Craig Bolton. Cleah had her 4th birthday on March 11 and Kenneth would soon be 2 on August 8. Already in the fourth year of a seemingly unending Depression, two children to a couple seemed enough to support. The abortion which had been strongly recommended was rejected by both my parents. So, I increased the population in the United States of America from 122,775,046 to 122,775,047.

The doctor misspelled my name on the birth certificate, Donna Fay (the masculine spelling). The first lesson I learned from a mistake by a man.

And so my life began with the country in an economic mess. The hottest day of the year. The doctor not present. Two kids ahead of me in the food line. The only blonde child with royal blue eyes, the other two had brown hair and eyes. What chance in the world did I have? I had every chance for I was born An American Woman. Translated, the origin of my name is LADY. It is still questionable whether I've lived up to my name, but there may still be time.

The century was one-third gone by the time I entered along with a new president, Franklin D. Roosevelt. Since there was already a boy and girl in the family, gender was not important. It was only important that another democrat increase the population. It's the past two-thirds of the 20th century I want to share with my grandchildren and their generation to know of the events and choices that shaped my life. The lives of those who came before me and their decisions had a great impact on me and are well documented in history books.

Within two months of my birth we moved from the family farm on South 55th Street and Hoover into Wichita where Dad had a bread route to a number of grocery stores giving us more financial security than many who were standing in breadlines for food. One day the baker forgot to sift the flour and the mouse droppings were ingredients in the bread. The bread orders were cancelled as was Dad's job. In some ways the mouse droppings were timely.

Within a few days Dad went to work for Sedgwick County Road Maintenance. Although the pay was better there was still little money for luxury items like portraits. To have a picture of me, Mother entered me in a Beautiful Baby Photo Contest.

The photographer came to the house and poised me in my best print dress in the ever-lasting-wing-back-blue chair. He made me laugh and I won the contest, which was a large hand-painted photograph. Mother had her picture but thereafter she would let my heavy-hard-to-manage mop of blond hair grow long. The photographer told her it was my royal blue eyes that won.

In the next year, we moved from North Martinson to a better home on South Custer. During the move I got thirsty and drank some kerosene, causing my first visit to a hospital and to have my stomach pumped. Afterward, drinking was never a problem in my life.

In that same year, Mother gave birth to another boy, Raymond. She had delivery problems and he was a small sickly child. Not only did she have his illness to contend with but I came down with Scarlet Fever. I was quarantined in a bedroom and Dad was relegated to the basement so he could continue to work.

In this house and time is my earliest memory as confirmed by Mother and my sister. First is the memory of being in a bathroom unable to reach the oblong door knob with an embossment image of a little girl. Mother finally heard me crying and unlocked the door to rescue me. She believed that to be the first of my fear of being in close spaces, pronouncing me thereafter claustrophobic. I was about 2 years old and that phobia has not changed.

The second event that happened during lockdown was one never to be forgiven. I played near the window wanting to be outside. Grandma and Grandpa Craig came to visit and Grandpa stayed at the window to play with me. To this day I remember his funny faces.

Also, while playing alone, I was adventuresome and got into the Christmas decorations stored under the bed. The family had some lovely glass red birds with long white feather tails. I pulled the birds' tails out and tried to eat them, demolishing the birds. The destruction was most upsetting to the family. A void would be at the top of our Christmas tree for years where the red birds should have been perched. Fifty years later Cleah gave me two ceramic birds for my tree to confirm her long overdue forgiveness of my transgression against the originals. She gave me one, then several years later the second, forgetting she had already given me one of forgiveness. Had she not carried the resentment for decades, I probably would have no memory of my first destructive action.

At that same house, two Nazarene women called on Mother inviting us to their church. We went. I thought it funny when a woman came dancing down the aisle singing. Dad gave me the eye to stop laughing. Then I became bored when the sermon started. I'd heard a number of men mumble "Amen" in agreement with the preacher. I dozed off to sleep. A man behind me agreeably shouted "Amen" and I awakened in shock shouting to the top of my voice "Amen" a bit louder. Dad quickly picked me up to hush me and firmly placed his hand across my mouth. If we continued to attend, I don't recall it but have been told that ended our attendance at the Nazarene church. At least Dad's and mine.

When I was 3 we moved to a house on South Seneca with more land, a small barn and chicken house. The day we moved, it was my responsibility to rock Raymond in Grandpa Craig's large baby cradle and keep him entertained, a seemingly lifetime assignment. It kept him corralled and me out of the way.

It was an eventful year for me. Because of Raymond's poor health, I stayed with Grandma and Grandpa Craig much of that fall. I had a chronic ear infection and in December of my third year was the worst.

Christmas was always celebrated at home with our immediate family. And, since all of our extended family lived in the area, we usually were at both grandparents' home on Christmas Day. We had Santa gifts at home in the morning with stockings hung in different places, depending on the house we were living in at the time. We could always anticipate a large apple, an orange and hard jellyfilled, colorful candy, maybe a new dress and a toy from Santa. I wondered at the time how Santa got the dress I saw

Mother making for me.

On this Christmas Day I was lying on the self-pillow day bed in the over-sized dining-setting room where I could watch the festivities and enjoy watching the multi-colored lights on the tree in the living room. Uncle Ralph, Aunt Mildred's husband, came to hold and cuddle me while Grandma poured warm oil in my ear. The heat caused the abscess to burst and matter spewed from my ear. I thought my head had exploded and my brains were draining out on the pillow.

Cousins cried at the sight, making matters for me worse for I thought I was like Humpty Dumpty and would not be put back together again. They were rushed away into the living room to admire the tree.

Uncle Ralph assured me that I was going to feel better as he washed my face and combed my near-to-the-waist mass of curly blond hair. He picked me up and carried me to the living room and talked to me about the glass ornaments and an angel hiding on a top branch near the window. He told me to always remember the angel for she would care for me just as he was doing when he could not be with me. I named her Ralph.

Dad was outside helping Grandpa with a chore as he always seemed to do regardless of the day. Mother was in the kitchen with aunts helping prepare large amounts of food with all the traditional trimmings to go with the huge browned roasted turkey ready for carving. My favorite dish was Grandma's oyster dressing, a specialty and served only with the Christmas dinner.

I had to keep my draining, messy ear on the pillow. Mother brought me some turkey and the oyster dressing and first-to-be-served date pudding dessert. When that came, I didn't mind not eating with others.

We cousins, seven at the time, usually ate at scattered folding tables while the men, great-grandmother

Sampson and our three great-aunts took the first table seating in the spacious dining room. The table was usually round but leaves had been added to convert it into an oblong table to seat 12 people. After the first table seating, the second came. Aunts would clear the table, wash the dishes, reset the table and dish up fresh or reserved portions of food for themselves and enjoy a similar feast. The only difference between the two tables was the amount and topics of conversation. Men spoke one at a time, discussing. Women talked, not one at a time.

After dinner everyone pitched in to clear the table, sweep the floor, and rearrange the chairs so all could gather for the name-drawing gift exchange. Grandparents gave gifts to each of us. Aunt Myrtle gave boys shirts and we girls had at least two pieces of fabric for a school dress and a "Sunday" dress. Aunt Lilly would provide a religious book for each of us from "Grandmother Sampson's House."

Our gifts from whomever had our name were most often sensible, useful items, a scarf with mittens, a heavy sweater for school, colors and coloring books and for me, almost always paper dolls. Aunt Billie once made a very pretty red-with-large-white-leaves bathrobe for me from feed sack fabric she and Mother had saved from the 100-pound chicken feed bag. Nothing was ever wasted, sometimes a sad reality.

Dad's family was large and just being together for Christmas was a celebration. Grandma had a simply decorated tree and on it was a gift for each member of the family. Since Dad had seven sisters and three brothers, all with wives and children, it was nothing to have 50 people scattered in the kitchen, dining and living rooms in the farm house.

The big day at the Craig family was Christmas. The fun day at the Bolton family was Easter. Grandma would color a big basket of eggs and hide them around the farmyard for us to search for hours on the "hunt." The boys had the advantage for they were usually in overalls with dress shirts, we girls were still in our church Easter dresses.

After Grandma and Grandpa Bolton moved to a smaller home on South Pattie, it really got crowded. Regardless of the number showing up on Christmas night, there were always ample kolaches and klobaski. And, always on the back of the stove a large pot of coffee. Yes, with enough milk, we all got a cup. I don't remember when I had my first cup and I hope someone will give me a last sip when I take my last breath on this earth.

These Christmas traditions continued in the same pattern from childhood into adulthood. From one year to the next, this was the family gathering to be cherished for the next year one of the chairs might be vacant.

All too soon that year, 1936, I was to learn what an empty chair meant and experience death for the first time. In the spring of 1936, Grandpa Craig's mother, Eliza Lucinda Kessler Craig, died. She had come to Kansas in 1872 from Roanoke, VA and had land homesteaded in her name. She married a Presbyterian Scotsman, Archibald Craig, and settled on a farm at Tyler and Central in Delano township. Their comfortable farm home is recorded in the early history of Sedgwick County.

In 1909 she built a new home and moved from the farm on Tyler to 1521 Fairview.

We had been to visit her in that lovely big home several times while she was ill that winter. While adults gathered at her bedside, we kids played on the concrete wall with the horse-head post in the front yard. I fell and really scrapped my knee. Uncle Ralph to my rescue once again. He cleaned the wound then tied his white handkerchief around my knee like a head scarf and with his pen drew on a face with the bruise the red lips. It was so funny. He was so gentle and kind. My handsome angel had healed me again and I adored him.

The next time I was in that house, there was no laughter. Eliza Lucinda was lying in state in the parlor. It was spring, just when the iris were starting to bloom. It was the first time I saw my Grandfather cry. I started to cry and Mother's cousin Frank Kessler picked me up and carried me out of the house to the flower garden in the back yard. He told me if I listened to the birds I could hear violins. I didn't know what a violin was.

This also was the first of many times I would make the trip to Jamesburg, the family cemetery on the Kessler farm near 21st and Tyler Streets. We went to my grandparents for a meal after the services, and then it didn't seem so sad. Except for the gifts it was almost Christmas again.

Aunt Mildred played the piano and Uncle Ralph sang hymns with anyone who wanted to join in the celebration of Eliza with her favorite songs. Of course, I joined in even though I didn't know a word.

That fall the devastating call came that Uncle Ralph had been killed while working on a KG&E electric line in Cherryvale, Kansas. My dear Uncle Ralph, how could this happen to him? By training a concert pianist, it was Depression years and he'd taken a job with Kansas Gas and Electric Company and lucky to find work of any kind. He and Aunt Mildred had no children. He always made me believe I was his special little girl. I learned a tough lesson, what it was like to love someone and have them killed, never to see them again, not die old and sick as Grandma Eliza. Maybe it was "her time." It was not his. He left the angel with me, just as he said he would.

The Christmas of that year, Grandpa put only 11 chairs at the first seating at the table. He seemed to sense that I was feeling the absence. He picked me up and carried me to see the angel on the Christmas tree, then to his rocking chair by the desk and trotted me on his knee singing

"Pony Boy" as he had done every evening before I went to bed in the winter before when I had the ear infection and stayed with them.

As he'd rock and trot, I'd laugh and Grandma would admonish him for treating me as a tomboy. She would remind him I was a girl. He'd say, "I love to hear her laugh." That is how I came to have my only nickname, Happy. The name he used for me all my childhood, when Grandma wasn't within earshot. On into adulthood when he would call me Happy, a vision of the angel would come clearly to mind.

By the next fall, while still living on Seneca, I started kindergarten at Stanley Elementary. In the first months of school I had chicken pox and had to stay home almost missing the Thanksgiving program. I was a pilgrim. While I was confined to home, Mother made a black dress and white apron for me from real fabric, not paper. Since I had the best costume, I got to be on center stage for the program, sweeping the floor and saying a poem. I liked performing on stage. I also liked having Mother's smile of approval.

I didn't finish Kindergarten for in the spring we moved to South Gordon with more land, a bigger barn for more milking cows which included milking stanchions, and two chicken houses. It was a delightful two-story house with lots of space for our growing family. Dad seemed to keep moving us to more acreage as we grew and could do more chores. Our work in the garden, milk barn and caring for animals and fowl provided better and more food for the family. Tough, if we didn't care for our assigned chores. We did them.

When rain did not fill the cattle tank for drinking water for the cows and calves, Kenneth and I had to pump water with the pitcher-pump. Although he was large enough, only the long handle permitted me to take my turn.

We each were to take 1,000 strokes for each turn. At that time I could count to a 100 but I didn't understand how to count to a thousand. That was about to change. Kenneth would count and pump to 799, then came 1,000. When I was pumping and he was counting, something was added. There were numbers of 800 and 900 before 1,000. When realization struck me, I chased him with a hoe around the barn. Not only did he teach me about numbers, he taught me that he was older, bigger, and could run faster. He'd always be ahead of me.

At the front drive there were large white concrete pillars higher than the fence supporting the crisscross wood in an attractive design. It also had very large elm trees, beginning at the drive, with interlocking branches for a couple of city blocks lining the pasture fence. By this time Kenneth had become very inventive in providing us with unique handmade play equipment.

He tied a heavy rope on a sturdy limb and attached a gunny sack filled with straw to the other end. It provided a grand swing. We could run, jump on it and maneuver it to a height to catch a high limb releasing us into the next tree. Kenneth, Raymond and I were agile enough to transfer from tree to tree the length of the two blocks and back to the rope. We'd grab the rope and very carefully, hand-over-hand, lower ourselves back to the ground.

When our grandparents came to visit they asked Mother where we were, she said, "someplace in the trees." Grandma let Mother know she was unhappy for fear we would fall. Grandpa said regrettably he didn't know he had monkeys for grandchildren.

That is, except Cleah. Only once did she mount the swing and that was a disaster. She took off the wrong way swinging perpendicular not parallel with the trees. She started swinging out over the gravel road. As she did, Dad's bridge gang came driving down the road to drop him off from work. As she reached the highest point in the swing, she was above the cab of the truck. The rope broke in that instant and she flew to the other side landing in the ditch. She landed as she was swinging, her feet and legs straight out in front of her with her bottom clutching the straw-filled gunny sack.

Dad yelled to the driver, "Stop, there goes Cleah!" He jumped from the truck to pick her up and found her not hurt but screaming to the top of her lungs.

The three of us were ordered out of the trees. That lasted until everyone's attention was diverted to other more important work and we went back to the trees when we had time to play.

The years of the late '30s were not all doom and gloom for us or most people we knew. By this time Dad was a foreman for the Public Works Administration (WPA), a Roosevelt New Deal program, employing men to build everything from park benches to bridges. Dad was self-educated, having only a 6th grade education. He taught himself to read blueprints from any angle, landing a foreman job. He supervised the work of more than 300 men. Money was tight, but times were better for us.

We had a newer car, a 1935 black Chevrolet. We began going to the West or Civic movie theaters on Wichita's west side. We went frequently enough to catch the sequels of Zorro, the Lone Ranger, Hopalong Cassidy, Batman and anything else that was playing. Dad liked westerns and comedy. Mother liked history and newsreels giving us worldwide news in motion pictures, mostly what was happening in Europe with a man named Hitler.

Dad and Grandpa were active in local Democrat politics. Dad and his friends decorated a car with red, white and blue pom-poms to drive in the big parade being planned. I helped push the crape paper into chicken wire stretched over the wood frame mounted on the car. During the 1936 campaign, President Roosevelt was coming to Wichita for a city parade and a speech at Lawrence Stadium.

As the President's car came down the drive at the stadium, he was giving Democrat Donkey pins. They were covered with clear rhinestones, one was bright green, the donkey's eye. I was on Dad's shoulders and he leaned me over for the President to give me a pin. I clutched it so hard I pricked my hand.

Grandma Craig was at Wesley Hospital unable to be with us. After the parade, we drove to East Wichita to see her. We kids stayed in the car under Cleah's watchful eye while Mother and Dad went to visit her and tell her of seeing President Roosevelt. As Dad got out of the car, he took my donkey pin from me to give to Grandma. I cried. I don't know what ever happened to the pin; I could still cry.

I mentioned how the movies progressed, even more for us, we listened to the radio. Electricity was changing how America lived. The big chore of the laundry was now done with an electric washing machine. Hot water and a wringer to expel most of the water from fabric revolutionized this task for most women and it was no different for Mother. Items being washed in soapy water in the machine tub were placed between the wringers into a large aluminum tub with cold water for rinsing. Swing the arm around the tub and wring the cold water from the clothes, dropping them into a basket for hanging on an outside clothes line … rain or shine, hot or cold weather, with bird droppings and leaves blowing into everything, flapping dry in the Kansas wind. It beat the washboard and wringing overalls by hand. I liked wash day and playing in the cold rinse water.

The radio provided us great listening pleasure. We listened to Jack the All-America Boy, Gracie and George Burns, Amos and Andy, Jack Benny, Mystery Theater, all the great talent broadcasting mostly from New York. My favorite on Saturday mornings was "Let's Pretend." A different fairy tale was told each week and my imagination helped get me through the morning cleaning chores. It took me forever, according to Mother, to "simply sweep the floor."

During times I stayed with Grandma the only doll I had was a cloth doll with an embroidered face and yarn hair that Mother had made for me when I had Chicken Pox. What I wanted was a real bear like the one in the picture in Grandma's magazine. She saved magazines from year to year to reread them and mark favorite recipes. She knew which year, which month had what favorite recipe in it.

One had a picture I really liked. It was of a toy called a Teddy Bear. It had legs that moved, was warm and fuzzy. One day after my nap and she wasn't in the room, I carefully tore out the picture. I put it in an envelope from her desk to give to Santa when we went to see him at the department store. I told all my friends at school that Santa was going to bring me the bear. He didn't.

When the teacher asked us to tell what Santa brought us, everyone had trains, trucks, jump ropes, jacks, tinker-toys, Lincoln building blocks, and every girl seemed to have a really big doll! Some of the kids had brought their gifts to school for "show and tell." I had nothing to show or report so I said, "I got a real bear."

When Mother came to pick us up from school, my teacher met her at the car. She told Mother she didn't think it was safe to have a real bear with children around. She then told Mother that I'd told the class I got a real bear. Dumb lady. It was the real Teddy Bear that I wanted and did not get, not just a picture of one. Not a real live bear.

When we got home, Mother took me aside for Cleah, Kenneth and Raymond were laughing their fool heads off that I'd told everyone we had a real live bear at home. She shook me for telling something that was not true. I could not tell her about the picture from the magazine for Grandma had questioned everyone about the hole where someone had dared to "rip up" a page along with part of a very good recipe. I took the punishment, the teasing from siblings and learned my first lesson about real trouble.

My trouble was minor compared to those caused by the dust storms we were having. Wind blowing so much dirt you could not see beyond the porch. No rain with it. This was during the dustbowl in Kansas and many of the prairie states. We walked from Eureka school down West Street a half mile to McCormick Street, then another half-mile past Mount Carmel Convent to Gordon Street, turning a couple of blocks to reach home. Most of the time it was a fun walk. I usually walked with Bonnie who was our neighbor and in the 8th grade; I was in the first. I could keep up with her and she made me walk fast.

Sometimes I walked with Kenneth. Raymond was not yet in school and Cleah, now in the 7th grade, walked with her boyfriend, Mr. Miller. If the weather was too bad and Mother had the car, she came to get us. Years later when Vern Miller became Attorney General for Kansas, I teased him about giving me a nickel bribe to walk ahead of them.

I stayed home some days for the dust was too bad for me to go to school when Mother didn't have the car. One very bad day, Cleah left with her friend Mary Lou and rode home. Kenneth was out in the storm walking by himself. He'd been given a leather pilot's hat with goggles for Christmas. He had that with him and Mother only hoped he was wearing it. Time came when even in the dust storm he should have been home. He was not and Mother was crying for she had no way of finding him. She didn't have the car and she could not leave me and Raymond to look for him. And, she didn't know for sure where he was. Cleah had gone home with Mary Lou.

He had taken a short-cut across the Mount Carmel Convent grounds, been blown over and rested by a very large tombstone in their cemetery. When he regained his strength, he walked down the railroad tracks which led him to our pasture and barn which he could find. He was exhausted as he came into the house.

His cap looked like it had been sandpapered and his goggles were specked by the sand blowing into his face. Mother had him take a bath, change into one of Dad's big shirts and gave him some hot chocolate, which was not given to the rest of us. She stopped crying and that night worked it out with Dad that when it was badly storming, she'd take him to work and keep the car. Dad had no choice but to agree.

The dust storm was more damaging to our lives than the Depression. With a well-weeded and hoed garden we usually had ample food for the summer and fall and canned for winter-into-spring. Not that year. Dust covered the garden and anything else in its path. In spite of the hardship it created, we always had something to eat. We never knew where Mother got all the beans. Dad's favorite line at the time was, "When Boltons eat beans, Boltons eat beans." He made a believer of us.

I started kindergarten at Stanley; first grade was at Eureka I, north of Maple on West Street. Miss Clay was our teacher and there were 99 students who showed up for her class. There was no pre-registration; Mother took care of that on the first day of school. We sat two to a desk until they found another class room and another teacher. There remained 49 students in my class.

Miss Clay had a long ruler and could reach out to tap the desk if there was any whispering. She was totally no-nonsense.

She proved it. She announced to us on that first day that there was no such person as Santa Claus, that was our parents doing for us. Not only that, but there was no such animal as an Easter Bunny. Rabbits do not lay eggs. I was crushed. People aren't supposed to lay eggs either but she sure did that day.

I told Cleah what she said and she told me to talk to Mother. I ran all the way home rushing into the house yelling at the top of my voice to Mother the devastating words from Miss Clay.

We sat at the kitchen table. Mother sent Kenneth and Cleah out to play and get Raymond out of ear shot. She poured a glass of milk and gave me some ginger snap cookies. I knew at the moment it must be true for she was giving only me a treat.

She confirmed the news. Referring back to the Bear story in my earlier life, I told her I thought she should go straight to bed for telling me something untrue. She said that sounded good to her but she had to start dinner for the family. So much for my dishing out punishment to her.

Raymond came in and grabbed a cookie from my plate. Looked at me, raised his bushy eyebrows under that shock of white hair and said, "So you finally found out about Santa and the Easter Bunny. Hahahahahah!" The miracle he lived to adulthood was not because he was sickly.

Into the second grade we moved to a larger pasture, smaller house on Hoover Street. It was further from Eureka school but we were all older and could handle the mile walk to school, especially if we walked across the railroad trestle across the Big Ditch. They had found a small alligator a short distance from the bridge, a pet someone lost. We thought there could be more so we tread lightly crossing, stepping on each rail tie carefully.

A couple of horses came with the pasture and barn. We were so excited about getting to ride. Kenneth got the bridle on the sway back mare. Her back dipped so much that both Cleah and I could sit in her cradle not needing a saddle, we thought.

We were near the end of the pasture when Cleah got tired of plodding along so slowly. Forgetting that I was mounted behind her, she reached to slap the horse on the rump but missed and hit my bare leg. The sound frightened the horse causing her to make a quick turn and run faster than we imagined she could go to the barn. We didn't go riding together on her again.

Miss Davis was nicer than Miss Clay but she only had 42 of us in her second grade room. By today's standards, it is a wonder she could teach as much as she did. But, we learned to read, practice penmanship, do arithmetic problems, memorize short poems and songs. Most of all, we learned to say the Pledge of Allegiance to the Flag of the United States of America. And, there I met the first girl friend I ever had, Marilyn; she lived on a farm a mile from us.

Life was harder for we had more animals and a larger garden to tend. Dad was still working building bridges with his large work force. He was building the twin bridges at Lake Afton, near Goddard, and had to stay out on the job to keep the water pumped out of the building area. As our size increased, so too did our chores.

An occasional stay with Grandparents became a real treat. When it was my turn to stay, we went to the Civic to see the first movie I remember from start to finish – "The Wizard of Oz" with Judy Garland. I had heard her sing "Somewhere Over the Rainbow" on the radio and had learned most of the song.

Sunday when the family came out for dinner I was so excited to tell them about the girl from Kansas, the tornado and how it changed from black and white to color. They didn't believe me when I told them about the rainbow in color. So I walked over by Grandpa, stood by his chair, and sang every word of the Rainbow song. Tears rolled down his and Dad's face.

Grandpa told the folks I was telling the truth and they should let me take them to the movie to see for themselves. That's when I realized what a true friend he was to me.

Telephones, electrical gadgets, better designed cars, trucks, refrigeration, and "good American ingenuity" was changing how we lived and worked. That included women.

During this time many families had moved from farms into the city for work and a more comfortable life. It changed the family farm and the cities with the population switch. That included us. Mother had plenty to do taking care of the family and did not work away from home, but Aunt Mildred worked for the electric company after Uncle Ralph died. Aunt Louise worked at the new Stearman aircraft plant. The two of them always seemed to have nice homes and furniture in them, better clothes, a current model car and candy available everyday, if you could find it.

Two great-aunts were maiden school teachers and took great pride in their activities in the decades before when they had marched in downtown Wichita to assure the passage of the 19th Amendment giving women the right to vote. Both impressed upon us girls of our generation that we had an obligation to vote or those men would take away our right to vote from us faster than it had come. Their directives were just that. I have not missed voting.

The family took two trips, one in 1939, the other in 1940.

My first trip out of Kansas was to take Grandma Bolton to see her mother, Great-Grandmother Maria Vignati, in Perry, Oklahoma. It would be the only time I saw her. She was a small woman, laughed while she talked, speaking half English and half Czech. She was born in Brno, Moravia, and came to America as a young wife and mother of the first two of her five children.

We met lots of family I'd never seen before. Aunt Anna, her son, Ralph, and cousins who lived on a farm just out of town. It was there I had an introduction to home brew. I'd never smelled, tasted or seen anything like what that drink brought about. Many adults were gathered around a large kitchen table drinking from large glasses with handles. A big black car drove into the farmyard. I had been standing at the back of Dad's chair. I was pushed aside. The glasses were emptied in a bucket which someone rushed with out the back door. The table was pushed off the hand braided rug, a trap door on the floor opened, the bottles that had been on the table were placed in a wooden box under the floor, the rug pulled back into place with the table on top. A table cloth was spread, coffee cups filled, a big bowl of kolaches was placed in the center.

All this happened before my eyes and faster than I can tell the story. When the man in uniform came in the kitchen, he was offered food and coffee. He took both, looked around, stared at me as did everyone else. Cleah and Kenneth were not far away but he didn't even glance at them. Raymond was on Mother's lap asleep.

I thought his look was an invitation to join him. I did. I took hold of his jacket and said, "We have some new puppies outside; Would you like to see them?" He left the house with me. Made him an offer he couldn't refuse.

On the way home, Dad was laughing with Grandma about how well I had escorted the visitor outside. Dad was driving, Kenneth was in the front seat next to Grandma. Mother had Raymond on her lap, I was squashed in the middle, with Cleah next to the right window.

On the way, Dad saw a cotton patch and pulled off the road so we could see what it looked like in the field with white balls hanging off of each plant. We picked some growing in the ditch for Show and Tell at school.

I tried to change places with Kenneth but it didn't

work. He was bigger and faster than I, so back to the middle seat in the back I went. It was a hot day and as we drove, even with the windows open, I could smell the home brew Dad and Grandma had drunk. Closer to home my cotton turned brown as I turned green. Only a quick stop would relieve the pain. I don't ever recall throwing up before. I didn't know I could hold so much. Neither did Mother.

Show and Tell wasn't all it could have been. I was told to strictly keep my remarks only on the cotton, as brown as it was. The rest of the story about the officer would have been a lot more interesting.

Our second trip was to visit Aunt Marie, Mother's sister, and Uncle Ted who had moved to Ada, Missouri. They had built a one-room plank house with a kitchen in one end, dining-living area in the middle and curtained off at the back was their bedroom.

Mom and Dad slept on the leather sleeper sofa, the four of us kids on blanket and pallets on the wood floor. Aunt Marie was a good country cook, had a wonderful vegetable garden surrounded by flowers, and their two cows and a few chickens produced plenty of milk, cream, cheese and eggs for ample meals.

During the day we went to see the lumber mill Uncle Ted was operating with his brother. The large waterfall behind the house supplied everyone in the area with fresh drinking water and the mill.

Kenneth, Raymond and I had a great time exploring the wooded area around the house while Cleah visited inside. It was during those days I decided that before I died I would see real mountains all over the world. For Christmas I asked for a world globe bank and got it. I started saving to travel.

When we got home, things in the country were changing.

More legislation had been enacted in Washington to help people, but also control them. The Social Security Act's major promoter was Eleanor Roosevelt. She, more than any first lady before her, became an activist and spokesperson for the President. Many thought it was mostly because he was confined to his wheelchair due to his polio. I was brought up to think she was filling her duties as she prescribed them. She wrote her own job description and dared anyone to challenge her authority. Grandma and Mother thought she should stay home with her husband and control her wild kids.

The vote, the New Deal and Eleanor were credited with opening the doors for women, especially in high government positions. Opportunities began opening in other professional fields but there were still few women accepted into medical, law or engineering colleges. A few slid in through the side doors but none entered the front door of major universities.

As the 30s ended and a girl was asked, what do you want to be when you grow up, about all she could answer was: a nurse, a teacher, a librarian, a seamstress, a store clerk or a housewife.

Adult talk was changing. Some of Roosevelt's social programs would survive: Social Security, housing reform, income taxes. His strength was weakening as he pushed to appoint and change the makeup of the Supreme Court and at the same time manage the opposition to the war raging in Europe.

Dad brought the reality of the war to us as he gathered us around him one evening and read an article in The Wichita Eagle. A family was trying to leave Czechoslovakia, the country of Moravia and the place of his mother's birth. Cousins were still living there.

The family was loaded into hollowed out overstuffed chairs and sofa with furniture piled all about them and covered with straw. They were stopped by German soldiers and shots were fired into the load. The mother and father were inside the sofa. Two children were curled in the bottom of the chairs. The father had only slight wounds but all escaped.

He then told us our country might be going to war and he wanted us to know what was happening in the world. If the draft would be increased he might have to go to the Army. He had been too young for WWI but might not be too old if war came to the United States.

Mainly because of the threat of war, President Roosevelt was elected to his third term of office. However, officials in Sedgwick County changed and the commissioner Dad had supported publicly, lost. As new men took office in January of 1941 they appointed new work supervisors of their own party. Dad lost his job.

It was a traumatic experience for all of us.

2. Kansas and Me Under the Rainbow

This decade of the '40s was not looking so good. Not only was there excited talk about the war and if the country would get in it or stay out, but Dad had no job, our home had been sold so we had to move, and we still had two more months of school.

Miss Craven was my third grade teacher, a small, pretty dark haired woman and so patient with all of us. I really liked her and I had lots of girl and boy friends. If everything else was going to hell-in-a-hand basket as Grandma said it was, my life was not. It didn't take long for me to learn that I had little say in the matter.

Dad took a temporary job at the Municipal Airport building the new runway for the larger planes that Stearman-changed to Boeing-was beginning to build. They were building bombers.

That job lasted only a few months to the completion of the project. He kept the blueprints and pictures from the site for years. After his death I gave the originals to the Wichita Air Museum for they contained the original drawings of the utilities under the runway. A most appreciated gift.

Dad was offered a supervisory job with the Federal Highway Department building the Yukon Highway to Alaska. We would be going with him. We were all in anticipation of a great adventure, including Mother. His parents approved anything he did. Mother's did not. Both grandparents threw a royal fit when they got the news.

We were going to have to move anyway and it would be a good job for Dad. It would only be for two years and then we'd be back. I looked forward to having a real fur coat.

At the final hour, they asked Dad for his high school

diploma, a prerequisite for the job they had not mentioned. That ended his new job and my dream. No fur coat.

After that, Dad decided to go back to farming and never to be placed in a position to be fired from a job not because of what you didn't know but because of a piece of paper.

Just when everyone else was beginning to come out of the Depression, we were headed straight into it.

A small farm on West Harry across the road from where Aunt Billie, Mother's sister, lived was soon to be available. We moved in to stay with Grandma and Grandpa Craig for two weeks while Dad finished another project at the airport and the house vacated. Dad would take over the farming from Grandpa, add 12 cows to his eight to increase the herd and sell milk. We would do the milking and get two-thirds of the income. The same with crops.

We moved in March of 1941 and started school in a one-room country school, Daisy elementary, 1-8 grades. I was finishing the 3rd grade, Cleah the 8th. After being in class with 40 to 50 students, I now had one classmate. Joan Lies, who became a lifelong friend.

Even though we kids were getting bigger, the houses kept getting smaller. This one had a large kitchen, large dining-living room and three small bedrooms, but no bathroom. We had a two-hole outhouse, bathing on the back porch. No three minute baths now, thirty seconds would do or in the winter icicles would form in your hair. A pitcher-pump in the kitchen with floor to ceiling cabinets made life more livable.

We began going to Harmony Presbyterian Church which had been founded by early settlers including Great-Grandpa Craig. We usually were in attendance but because of the news coming on the battery operated radio, we were glued to it to hear the astonishing reports.

In the midst of listening, Grandpa Craig came wheeling in the farmyard, jumped out of the car yelling, we've been bombed. Dad had him come in to sit at the table to have coffee and pancakes with us while he gave a similar report to what we'd just heard.

WWII had begun. On Sunday, December 7, 1941, the Japanese had bombed Pearl Harbor. If that weren't enough, on Thursday, December 11 came the news that Hitler and his Nazi Germany had declared war on the United States. Much pressure had been brought about to not enter the European war. Hitler's declaration and sinking of the flagship would be responded to with full force. The war effort began.

Grandma and Grandpa Bolton were going to move from the farm on South Hydraulic to a smaller home on South Pattie which they had purchased. They had three acres, could still keep animals and have a garden. Before moving, Cleah and I went to spend the week with them. Aunt Betty took us to the corner filling station to get a soft drink or a candy bar, mine was always a Grapette or a Tootsie Roll. That was the only time I spent a week with them. We visited often, usually on Sunday afternoon, with most of the family gathering for coffee and whatever Grandma had baked in great quantity. She usually baked two big cakes and 6 pies at a time.

We knew many German people, some so new to the country they were struggling to speak English. With the war coming, they learned the language fast.

More questions than answers were all adults could talk about. Would Dad be drafted into the Army? How many and which of the uncles would have to go? Who would do all the farm work?

At that age, I had a way of focusing on my world and what impact all this might have on me. Dad, Mother and Kenneth had gone to Grandpa's milk barn morning and night to milk by hand the now 25 cows. Raymond usually went with them to do what feeding he could reach; he had just turned 7. Cleah and I stayed home to do the housework and cooking. Sometimes we would go with the folks but we stayed in the house to help Grandma.

That could change. I prayed hard, Dear Lord, don't make me have to milk any cows. I fed the chickens, gathered the eggs, set the table, dried the dishes. I didn't have time to milk cows.

During the Christmas break, I was ordered to the milk barn with Kenneth so he could teach me my new assignment. What misery. He hobbled the cow, showed me how to sit on the three-legged stool, how to clean the cow's udder, what and how to pull on the cow's teats. Disgusting.

Poor guy, as hard as he tried he could not make me understand that you pulled down on the teat using the index finger first. I did not do it that way. I started with my little finger and pushed up, reverse to his motion. No milk came. That ended any milking assignment. But I had grown tall enough to clean the cream separator, a smelly but more agreeable task.

It was a valuable lesson taught early in life that there are some tasks at which you need not, even should not, become proficient.

Dad was not drafted because of his age; he was 39 and the cut off at that time was 36. He also had a farm deferment as others younger than he for raising food was classified essential work to the war effort. Our lives were much as everyone else. Uncle Gene, Dad's youngest brother, and Uncle Paul, Aunt Mildred's second husband, were drafted. Uncle Gene was a mechanic on a tank and Uncle Paul was a foot soldier with General Patton's Third Army.

We were caught still driving the '35 Chevy when they stopped making automobiles for civil use. Many essentials were rationed, gasoline, shoes (anything leather), ladies silk hose and under garments, sugar, meat and other stuff I didn't know about.

It seemed that everything that was not an essential

was not available to us. Kid things, toys, dolls and in general things to play with, were not on our want list.

Items packed in the boxes with breakfast cereal were real treats. An offer came in one for sterling silver birthstone rings. Mother ordered one for Cleah, an aquamarine, and me, a ruby. The settings were ornate and the stones were glass. To us, they were the real things. My first ring, worn only on special occasions.

I liked blue better than red. So occasionally I tried on Cleah's to admire it on my hand. I had done that just before going across the road to take water to Kenneth who was working in the field for Uncle Steve across the road from our house. I thought I'd taken the ring off and put it back in her dresser drawer.

While Kenneth was drinking his water, Mother and Cleah came running across the road. Cleah said I had her ring and Mother came to help her get it. It was not on my hand. All work stopped while we looked in the field, not there. We looked at the pump where I had gotten the water. Not there. We looked throughout the house. Not there. No doubt about it, I had lost Cleah's ring.

Mother took my ring and told me when and if I could be more responsible, I might get it back.

While crying myself to sleep, I retraced my steps and clearly remembered putting the ring back in its original little box. Why wasn't it there? Lesson learned, don't ever put on anything that does not belong to you.

When I was visiting Cleah in the care home for Christmas, 2007, I found the blue and silver cereal-box ring in a special jewelry box in her chest of drawers. I had given her very expensive aquamarine stud earrings for her 50th birthday with a note saying I was sorry I'd lost her ring when we were children. Not then nor ever did she tell me she had the ring all through the years.

We listened to the news, morning, noon and night.

Grandpa Craig had electricity so we could hear the radio more clearly without so much static. While cooking for harvest hands, Mother and Grandma listened to the Kate Smith show, some soap operas, and always the noon news to hear who would be the honored Soldier of the Day on KFH, a local radio station.

In the midst of clearing noon meal dishes, Grandma went to her rocking chair with dish towel in hand, crying, my little Raymond, my little Raymond. We rushed in to listen. Raymond Sampson, Grandma's nephew with the Army Airborne stationed in London, was the hero.

They were in the lead plane coming in after bombings, the landing gear would not come down and they didn't have enough fuel to get out of formation. Raymond crawled outside the airplane, hung by his knees and manually pulled the landing gear down into place so they could continue to lead the landing operation. In the process he was credited with saving many lives and planes of those following them onto the landing strip.

The war was real, our family was involved and emotions were raw, tense. Adult anxiety and conversations are well imbedded in my memory.

With everything else going on in the world, Uncle Steve decided to take his big truck to bring back a load of fresh peaches going to waste in Arkansas. He had mechanical problems and was very late getting to our house. As the four bushels of peaches were being brought into the back porch there was only a light from the small kerosene lamp in the kitchen.

Kenneth came running into the room, fell and cut a big gash above his eye that started bleeding something fierce. Mother ran to help him and Uncle Steve yelled at her to let the kid go and take care of the peaches. The sight of so many peaches, Kenneth's blood and being yelled at was too much. She started crying, then shaking. Dad came to help her and

Uncle Steve went to call the doctor.

The doctor arrived and told us Mother was exhausted and needed to rest, not do anything for a week and he would see her again. She was just worn out.

The next day Grandma Craig came to help Cleah and me can every peach that hadn't been eaten. We had a real assembly line that was in full swing for about 8 hours. For sure, the cellar shelves were full. Summer canning had provided ample winter stock of beans, beets, peas, pears, pineapple, tomatoes and anything else Mother could fit in a jar.

Mother had worked hard all of her life but was not a strong woman. She still went that winter to help with milking but that was cut back. She left more responsibility for the house when she was gone to Cleah for she was now in high school.

I raised a flock of 12 ducks from babies to harvest size. They were ready in time for Thanksgiving. Poultry was selling well.

Each grandparent bought a duck, Uncle Victor, Dad's brother took two, a neighbor bought two, leaving me with 6 to sell. Dad bought one, he'd also bought the feed for them. Mother had me help her pluck the feathers from them, dress them and we took them cleaned to the grocery story where Mr. Cohlmia bought all five. Before we left the store he had sold all five for $3 each. My first lesson in business, the middle man and profit.

I was rich. I had $12. Mother took Cleah and me shopping for winter coats. With my money I bought each of us heavy winter coats for $3 each. Mother's was gray, Cleah's was brown with a velvet collar and mine was heather blue of cuddly warm fabric. I had $3 left. I did my Christmas shopping for all the family with it and had 50 cents left for treats during the winter. I was so proud of my work and what I'd been able to do with the money I earned.

During the winter of 1943 the build-up of the armed

forces and supplies called for sacrifices from everyone, young and old, rich and poor. Reports of major battles won and lost were news subjects 24-hours a day.

For me, those battles didn't compare to the one about to take place at home. Mother had not had time to dress the chicken meant for supper before she left with Dad to do the milking. She told Cleah to do it. After she was gone, Cleah put the teakettle of water on to heat and ordered me out to slaughter the chicken. I told her I didn't know how to kill a chicken. That argument went on for a long time and I refused to go out in the cold, catch the chicken and kill it.

She heard the car coming in the drive. The folks were home. No dinner prepared. She got mad and threw the boiling kettle of water at me hitting my legs. I kicked her where it would hurt. At that moment Dad walked into the kitchen, saw me kick her, grabbed me, turned me over his lap and spanked me very hard. I was sent to bed crying, not from the spanking but from my burns.

The next morning, Cleah had left with her ride to go to Goddard High School, others to do the milking. I stayed in bed. Kenneth and Raymond went to school. Mother came in the room asking why I wasn't up and dressed to do the same. I told her my legs hurt too badly and that I didn't think I could put on stockings.

She pulled the cover back and was horrified when she saw my legs. She called to Dad, he came in looked and said the spanking he gave me could not have caused the injuries on my legs. I told them what had happened. Dad picked me up, carried me to the kitchen for Mother to doctor my legs. He sat down and cried. Never once did he ever strike me again.

That evening before Cleah got home, we left to go to Grandma's. The boys told her what had happened, but not to me. I then got a tongue lashing from her with instructions that she didn't ever want to hear of me disobeying Cleah again. I grabbed my coat and went to the car, curling up crying that none of them would ever hurt me again.

When the milking was finished they went to the house. Mother told the boys and grandparents what had happened and why my legs were wrapped. She asked where I was. Grandma said she thought I was with them, she didn't know. Grandpa came to the car, held me and confirmed that he would see to it that they would never hurt "Happy" again.

There was never an apology. I healed and the subject ended but the hurt did not. My relationship with Grandma and Cleah slipped, Grandpa's and Dad's raised.

We continued to gather on Friday nights with Aunt Billie's family and the Lies' family for card games and dessert, taking turns from house to house. On Saturday night, Cleah was busy watching the kids of the two families while the adults went dancing. Mother and Dad stayed home to listen to radio shows with the three of us.

Grandma had a heart attack that summer and Cleah went to stay to help with cleaning and cooking. Mother took the kitchen back and I had more outside chore assignments.

A good wheat crop and calves to sell and war prices for food in effect, life was better. A viable farm owned by long time family friends, four Nelson sisters, on West Central was available to rent so in August 1943 we moved again. This time the house was as big as the land. It was a two-story, seven-room house with four porches. The barn was really big and a windmill would pump all the fresh water we needed.

No electric lines had been built since before the war started, so still, we were without city comforts. Meaning we still had to use the outhouse. It was a typical colonial farm house, cold in the winter, cooled in the summer at the mercy of a Kansas breeze.

Mother and Dad were much happier. The milking

would be done at home. We had more space and more land would provide more income, but also more work. Cleah helped with the indoor chores of cooking and Kenneth was always out with Dad. Raymond and I each had chores, mainly working the garden, feeding livestock, and riding the two horses we'd moved with us.

One of my major tasks was "looking after Raymond." We spent a lot of time playing hide-and-go-seek for we had some great places to hide. His favorite was always the barn and especially the haymow where Dad stacked loose wheat straw to use to bed down the cattle in the winter.

Once, when I could not find him and after declaring him the winner, he did not appear in the upper doorway as usual. I ran to get Dad to tell him what was happening. I assured him Raymond was someplace in the straw. He took the handle of the pitchfork pushing it into the straw. Finally hit Raymond, pulled him out. He was dark. Dad blew into his mouth and slapped his chest. Raymond finally coughed and took a gasping breath. Dad cleaned him up, told me to go to the house but never to mention this to Mother if I wanted to live.

Had I not found Dad in time, Raymond would have died and it would have been my fault. To Mother, Raymond could do no wrong. I told him I was never going to play that game with him again, my life depended upon it. We began taking a walking stick with us and exploring the 160-acres until we knew every square foot.

We went to Plainview Elementary, another one-room school with 10 students from grades 1 to 7. Mrs. Whitby was our teacher and an artist. The first time I'd ever had any art lessons other than coloring from picture books. She also was impressed with my voice. Being alone in my class took on new dimension.

Mother usually drove us the 2 miles to school but we most often walked home. During the winter, in a deep snow, Kenneth would forge ahead making tracks for Raymond and me. His steps were so long we'd have to jump to hit them making it a game going home. Most often when we got there, Mother would have homemade bread with apple butter, cookies or even soda crackers and usually milk to drink before we did our chores.

Uncle Gene and Uncle Paul both landed in France on June 6, 1944, D-Day when the Allied Forces invaded Europe. Uncle Gene was in the third tank going ashore and, unlike most, made it safely.

Although the ongoing war in the Pacific and Europe dictated much of our lives, there was daily routine with farm chores and school that kept us going from sunrise to dark. And, thank goodness for dark. Since we didn't have electricity, work had to be completed outside by the time the sun went down. Summer was different, the sun was always shinning. And, the work was never ending.

Grandpa had kept his old Chevy car and had cut off the back, built on a bed to make a Jalopy for a runabout and to save his good car. I went every place with him. We hauled water to Dad and men working in the fields. We hauled feed to cattle, drove all over the pasture. We especially drove to Tyler Co-op where he would buy my choice of a Grapette or Orange Crush pop to keep me occupied while he visited with farmers about the wheat crop coming in to the elevator.

Kenneth sometimes drove the "J" in the fields and Raymond and I had a great time as he took us driving the equipment ruts.

On a rare occasion, Cleah came to Tyler with us. We'd had our treat and Grandpa his update from neighbors about the crops, the war and jokes I could not understand or didn't believe.

As we were leaving, he asked Cleah to take the pack of empty bottles into the store. She literally threw a fit, that all those men would be looking at her. Grandpa said, Oh, for

God's sake. Turned to me and said, Donna take the bottles inside. I did. When we got home, Cleah ran to tell Grandma what I had wanted her to do. Grandpa heard her and gave Grandma the straight story. Grandma sided with Cleah and I went outside, back to the "J." Cleah was almost an adult. Why was everything negative that happened to her my fault?

I enjoyed the time spent and lessons learned from being with Grandpa. He agreed to run for Sedgwick County's West District Commissioner position if he were unopposed in the primary election. The party gave him their nomination and I had a baptism in politics. I was out campaigning with him all summer and some on fall weekends. He won. His new position would have a major impact on my future.

At home, my assignment during the summer was to herd eight sheep along the road side and farmyard to feed them and keep the task of mowing to a minimum. I loved watching the big sky and would situate myself and the sheep where I would have no obstruction of trees for a view of the full big sky.

My favorite activity on long hot afternoons was to stretch out on the old quilt, watch the cloud formations and imagine them to be different objects or animals, sometimes strange looking people. I thought I knew some of the people. One was the weird guy who lived down the road from us.

Those were not the only formations in the sky.

As Boeing built and tested the B-29 bombers, they flew in formation over the farm. Dad would ask how many there were. I couldn't count them all before they would slip behind a cloud.

Kenneth taught me to just count the threes, then multiply them by the number of formations I counted. What a revelation. I started multiplying everything, from potatoes to eggs to chickens to clothes on the line. It was an exercise that kept me happy most of the summer and kept me from being bored with all the chores that increased by the week.

I was now tall enough and strong enough to gather eggs from the nests. Mother had a favorite setting hen, a mean Rhode Island Red. When I reached in to get her egg, she would peck me and draw blood. I threatened to put her in a pot every day.

When I was putting trash in the burn barrel I found a strainer with a handle that Mother had thrown out. Just what I needed. That hen was going to be managed. I could hardly wait to try my newly acquired weapon. I went to the hen house, slapped the strainer over her head, snatched the egg before she knew what hit her. She started squawking. Mother came running, sure I had done in her prize old red. I hid the strainer and handed Mother the big brown egg.

From that day on, we got along just fine. It was a good lesson–for in the years to come, I've seen the same glare from squawking females since.

Cleah was in high school and her life was different from ours in the one-room school. She was active in pep club, the mixed-chorus and she wore "better" clothes. She sold "War Stamps" and helped collect scrap metal for the war effort. She also got "sick" once a month. I did not know why and it wasn't explained to me.

During the year many men were killed in the war as they fought their way across France to Germany. Uncle Paul was with Patton's Third Army and we tracked the tough commander with a tough war job to do. All of the family helped Cleah with her war effort projects.

I had my own problem. As we were preparing for our Thanksgiving Day play at school, it was necessary for me to excuse myself to go to the bathroom. There was blood on me, on the floor and on the stool. I did not know what was happening.

After cleaning myself and the room, I called our teacher aside, Miss Swazye, and told her. She had turned 18 the week before so was sure an older woman could help me.

Very quietly she explained what was happening to me and why. She thought I was very young but not unusual. Now I knew why Cleah and been sick every month. If it was the natural order of a girl's life, what was the big secret?

Miss Swayze told me to talk to Mother and was surprised I did not know about such things. She gave me a spare belt and sanitary napkins to wear when it happened again. I didn't say anything to anyone about nearly bleeding to death with no warning.

Besides, everyone knew it was going to be a sad holiday season because of so many deaths in the war. The talk at Tyler with Grandpa was about the German army launching a massive attack and pushing our forces back, called the Battle of the Bulge.

Christmas with grandparents was teary. At Craigs, Aunt Mildred didn't know where Uncle Paul was and was sure she was going to be a widow again. At Boltons, Aunt Edna announced that she and Aunt Dorothy were going to New York City to be there when and if Uncle Gene came home.

The menu was the same, gifts as usual, but at night all Christmas lights had to be turned off because of the continued no lights curfew at night. Forced blackouts lasted the duration of the war. I checked to be sure my special angel was showing in the window so no lights didn't impact my celebrating the day.

We were attending Harmony Presbyterian Church, enlarged because neighbors came rather than driving into Wichita. Our Christmas Eve program was mostly music. I sang "Silent Night" and thought I was not doing it right for I saw Dad and Uncle Steve with tears streaming down their faces. Grandpa told me it was better than "Over the Rainbow." The nicest Christmas gift I received.

By spring, the war had turned in our favor with hopes of it soon being over. Then, one morning in April, the usual wake-up blast of Bruce Behymer at 6:00 on KFH radio station was subdued. The news was the announcement that President Roosevelt had died in Georgia. Harry Truman, the Vice-President, was now President and the nation mourned the death of a hero and speculated on how the incompetent man from Missouri was going to manage the war and lead the country. Some were sure we would be invaded for he didn't have the smarts of Roosevelt to keep the enemy at bay.

Grandpa told me he thought everyone was wrong about Truman. That he could be an excellent president for he would not put up with all the political nonsense that Roosevelt had. He told me to listen to every radio speech Truman gave and pay attention to how he managed. The folks let me stay up to listen to the broadcasts.

Within a month, Germany surrendered. Russia had a great deal to do with defeat and wanted to manage more than their share of the victory. Uncle Gene had been in the third tank when the Army marched into Germany, just as he had been going into France. He and Uncle Paul, with Patton's 3rd Army, would soon be coming home.

Kenneth was graduating from the 8th grade, Cleah would be in her senior year of high school. Uncle Gene came home safely and spent time with Dad talking about his future. Aunt Edna came to the farm with him and soon became my adult friend. He could not make plans for fear he was about to be shipped to the war front in the Pacific. He did not know where and four years away from home was enough and he wanted the war ended. But, he had no choice, jail was not an option.

Long battles had been fought that summer for places I had never heard of, nor could I find them on my small bank globe, Iwo Jima and Okinawa. In that time more than 4,000 Americans killed and 15,000 injured on Iwo Jima alone. Taking the Japan mainland would take thousands of more lives.

We were told that women and children were being armed to join the battle when the Americans invaded. Uncle Gene said the Russians would not enter the invasion so the amphibious landing would be up to the Americans.

He had landed in France but Japan would be totally different and he didn't think he would be coming home. We cried with him.

The not-to-be-trusted new president, he'd only been in office three months, made a major decision for the world and all of history. He warned Japan that we had a bomb of major destruction and it would be dropped if they did not surrender. They did not. On August 6, 1945, a B-29 bomber, the Wichita Boeing-built Enola Gay, dropped a single atomic bomb on Hiroshima. It killed or wounded more than 150,000 people and destroyed most of the buildings.

Not wanting to be left out of the glory of victory, the Russians entered the war on August 8. Kenneth's 15th birthday was celebrated thinking the war would come to an end. It did not. Japan refused to surrender. On August 9, Truman ordered the second bomb to be dropped. This time on Nagasaki. The Japanese leaders finally took him seriously and five days later came the official surrender.

America's best kept secret of the war, the Manhattan Project, was now public. Some believe the secret caused the beginning of the Cold War with Communist Soviet Union. Whatever was the beginning, it was the end of World War II. Uncle Gene stayed home.

Lives would be different. Kenneth would start to Goddard High School, the first Bolton male to have that opportunity.

As Wichita aero industry continued to supply military planes, they also stepped up production of civilian aviation. Flying Farmers, Flying Ranchers, Flying Clubs...all needed airplanes to feed the appetite of the hundreds of military-turned-civilian pilots. Uncles went to work at Beech, Cessna and Boeing. Aunts did not leave their work at the plants. Aunt Louise, who had helped make the upholstered seats for the Enola Gay, continued to work and became supervisor of the department. Aunt Mildred continued to work as secretary to the Gas Service manager. Both became role models for me.

Raymond and I would have a new teacher, Miss Roy. She was an artist and played the piano. She taught me to draw and paint pictures, my favorite was a very large "Rabbit in the Garden." Still in the family. We also listened to her classical music on the old phonograph someone donated to the school. She gave me books to read and a map of the nation so I could learn more about each state as we studied. I especially enjoyed the map and swore that someday I would visit every state, to see the mountains and swim in the ocean.

Our lives were beginning to come together again. We attended more activities at Goddard with both Kenneth and Cleah involved. Kenneth went out for football and played in the first game he or I ever saw. The same was true with basketball. We had seen lots of Dad's beloved baseball, but these were new and exciting sports to us. Kenneth spent a lot of time teaching us game rules.

The Goddard school district brought the little Planeview school into its district. At the same ceremony, Cleah graduated from high school, I from the eighth grade. It was a big night for us. Cleah had a purchased a navy blue dress and her gift was a gold watch. Mother and I designed my pink and white dress and I had white shoes with 2-inch wedge heels.

A week after graduation, Cleah went to live with Grandma and Grandpa Craig. She had an upstairs room at their spacious farmhouse. Grandpa got her a job as a clerk at the County Yards, the same place Dad had worked during his WPA days.

Her departure gave me the upstairs room to myself. I wanted it redecorated. It was as though Mother figured out for the first time she had two girls and two boys. I don't know who she'd thought I was. She also learned I was doing what comes naturally to girls and was shocked when I told her I had been going for almost two years. But, just every other month. Then she told me that was the same schedule with her and her mother. I'd thought I was very careful to wash my own clothing. Until Cleah left, I was safe.

There was no money for anything new for my room, but changes could be made. Grandma, aunts and Mother all purchased and saved the same feed sack design medium blue with small pink and beige flowers. We needed 12. Dad cut off the head of our iron bed, turning the foot to become the headboard, giving me the popular Hollywood bed. He cut a board the shape of a kidney to place on two orange crates to make a dressing table. The top was painted beige as was the woodwork. He cut off the back of an old dining chair and a thick pad was made to fit. Curtains and bedspread were made of unbleached muslin. The curtains, bedspread, vanity and bench were all skirted with the gathered feed sack material. The walls were papered with a-too-close-to-tell-it didn't-match wallpaper.

We completed my room after harvest in August and in time for me to start to high school with a room suitable for overnight guests.

On my birthday, Mother returned my confiscated ruby and sterling silver ring. I put it on and wore it daily throughout my years in high school. I still have it. Life was good for me.

3. Counting Boeing Bombers

After having been the only student in my grade for 5 years, it was a drastic change to have so many in school – 52. Some upper class members I knew from going to Kenneth and Cleah's activities. It did not take long until everyone in school was my friend. I was enjoying having a number of teachers and not having to help younger students with reading and math. Studies were all mine.

I was not as prepared for high school studies as I should have been. I had not had books or time to read as other students. It took half the year for me to catch up by doing extra assignments. I sang as did most students in mixed chorus but there were not many activities for us.

Kenneth drove the old Model A Ford and we picked up two children from two families on the way to Goddard. Seven of us packed in the small car and sometimes muddy roads made us late for school. By the next year Goddard had purchased school buses and we rode to and from school on the 12 mile route on the north side of Maple Street from Maize Road to west of Goddard and back. We left early and came home late.

Mother learned of a violin teacher and we still had the old violin Aunt Myrtle had given us for Cleah's lessons. Her playing had been short-lived. So, nothing would do but I start taking lessons. I found I rather liked doing what no one else in school could, they would not know how good or bad I was playing. Just keep the fiddle tuned and play simple songs.

My high school was routine for the time. As a Sophomore I did something out of routine and changed my life. Kenneth was playing football and as a Junior was on the first team. It irritated me that our scores were never in The Wichita Eagle. So, one day after a game when Mother went to Wichita to shop at Sears, I went to the newspaper office across the street.

I found the newsroom on the second floor. Don Granger, a court house reporter who was a good friend of Commissioner Craig, happened to be seated at a copy desk as I entered. I had gone to many baseball games with Grandpa and our seats were next to those of Don and his family.

Granger recognized me immediately, greeted me with great gusto introducing me to many by-line reporters. I was impressed. I told him I wanted Goddard's scores reported in the newspaper just like the big schools in Wichita. He laughed and said by all means they should be, took me over to the sports desk, introduced me to Pete Lightner, the sports editor and explained what I thought and why I was there. They winked at each other, then Lightner took my name, address and gave me an LD (Long Distance) number to call after the games, to ask for him and he would see to it that Goddard's scores were listed with those from Wichita schools. I thanked them both, clutching the note in my hand, left feeling on top of the world.

Little did I know at 15 I had just become one of five female sports reporters with a daily newspaper in the nation.

When I returned to Mother waiting in the car, I told her what I had done. She just laughed and said, you did what? I assured her I could do the reporting.

We stopped to drop off items and I told Grandpa what I'd done. He thought it was fantastic and would call Don when he went to the office and thank him for helping me. Grandma was less than pleased with me for being so forward. Grandpa was delighted, gave me a big hug and said he was very proud of me. He said he knew I could do it from the time I took the pop bottles back into the store without fussing, frequently reminding me of lessons learned in the past.

The next football game, I used the LD number, talked to Lightner and there not only was the score, but a short item about the game just as I had reported it. It worked. I worked for the first time.

In November, we drove to Warrensburg, Missouri, where Cleah was to be married to Don Palmer who she had met at work and been dating for the past nine months. Don was already there and Aunt Billie and Uncle Steve had taken Cleah and her things in the week before on their way to a family reunion.

I was to be her attendant. She wore a silver-green dress she and Mother had made. Mother and I found black dresses with sequin trim. I bought my first pair of really high heels, black leather pumps. By then I was 5'7" and towered over them both. Dad decided that dress was a "bit old" for me and suggested I not wear it in public again until next year, or maybe ten years from then. I felt good in it and surprisingly, Mother did not object.

I had a very good year. My friends, Nadine, DeeDee and Faye came to spend the night occasionally with me, my studies were going well, improvement on the violin was appreciated by Dad but not our dog. My assignment was broadening to reporting all sports and other schools. I'd spent a lot of time with Grandpa at the courthouse.

At that time I'd thought I'd like to be a lawyer. Grandpa took me to Judge Cline's office. He talked to me about what it would take for a girl to get into law school. He thought he could help me get into Washburn Law School in Topeka but it would be difficult for I would be taking up the seat of a male student. He didn't think there could be any scholarship available and it would be expensive. I knew money would be a problem even if I could make it. I left his office disappointed and angry. I did not like closed doors.

Grandpa talked to me about it and thought it best if I kept on the path of being a reporter, saying I was good at it. I'd been raised to think that when women were given the right to vote, other rights came with it. I'd been given the support and developed the belief that I could be or do anything I wanted. Not being so was a hard lesson for me.

My Junior year was Kenneth's Senior year and now Raymond joined us in high school. Cleah and Don moved back to Wichita where he went to work at Boeing and they announced to the folks they would be grandparents in the fall.

Farm income had improved enough for the folks to buy a half-section (320 acres) of land next to Vic Callahan's farm near Norwich, about 30 miles from where we lived. The summer of 1948 was one of the happiest for Mother and Dad.

It did not bide so well with me. I was helping Dad grease the inside auger in the bin of the combine. I crawled out, not knowing he had the machine jacked up. I jumped, hit the fly-wheel tire and was thrown about 20 feet into the sheep fence. For the next month I was off my feet with a badly sprained ankle and kept my foot in a bucket of ice.

I'd take a chair and my music stand outside and practice my violin by the hour. Dad finally asked me to move inside. He could not stand to hear the dog's yelping response another afternoon. He did not say anything about my playing. I would go over and over the same scales, rarely playing a recognizable tune. My teacher said I was not ready to start classical music and that's all I would be permitted to play. By spring I had a song to her liking I played at the school spring music program.

Since I couldn't do much work, I went with Grandpa as he gave speeches about the drainage ditch Wichita was planning to build in his district to divert the flood waters away from the Arkansas River. It was a major battle between West Wichita and the politically powerful East Wichita.

The Corps of Engineers came to the farm with maps

to talk to Grandpa who was home ill. They had a plan to build a big lake north to divert the water and provide a recreation area and provide a needed water supply for the city. It was all laid out on the dining room table.

That plan soon was changed. Wichita officials wanted it built faster. That could be accomplished by following the existing Slough running to the west of Wichita. The West opposed the direction for it would divide farms. Grandpa argued for his district and for three bridges to be built, one on Central, 13th and 21st streets. I listened to so many speeches I could give it for him. The East Commissioners said, "Hell Charlie, there will never be enough people west of West Street to warrant three bridges." The West lost. Only two bridges were built creating an awkward Windmill Drive to service both Central and 13th Street traffic. An unwise decision and hard feelings have never subsided.

Grandpa was finishing his four-year term on the commission and Grandma insisted he not run for another. She won. I would miss being with him and learning so much about government, politics and being in the know. What a great education his time of service had given me.

By the time school started I was off crutches but still had to have the elastic bandage on my leg as I slowly brought my muscles back into shape. I was anxious to be back in condition for basketball season.

Jay Hunter, an Indian Chief, was our coach. In a game we were winning by a large score, he motioned me to the bench. As I sat beside him, he said, Bolton, you may be broke someday but you'll never be flat busted. I turned red. Mother caught my expression and after the game was quick to ask what he said. I told her he complimented me. Had I told her what he said, I feared he would have been the first scalped Indian in Goddard.

What might have become unusual became routine during my Junior year. I played basketball, sang in the mixed-chorus, played the violin, reported sports to the newspaper. At the end of the school year we had a skip-day and went to Lake Afton. I went in the water with others. As I started to climb out of the water onto the boat deck, my classmate Bill offered me his hand. As I took it, I slipped, hitting my leg on the dock.

Down again. A knot started forming on my right shin bone. Every week Mother took me to see the bone specialist, Dr. Wier, to have it x-rayed every visit. The knot continued to grow, he put me back on crutches and told the folks it was not behaving as a cancer growth but it might be. I went through the same routine as the summer before. I was getting around very well on crutches, to climb stairs to go to bed, go wherever I wanted. I was also building up shoulder and chest muscles.

Long hair was vogue and my thick, dark blond hair grew in waves in length to my waist. I grew another inch to 5'8."

I went back for my senior year with my same routine except still on crutches. Without Kenneth, Nadine and Faye, things were different. We had many new teachers including a coach and American History teacher, Ed Stiggee. Girls basketball in the league was dropped. I was indifferent to the action for I couldn't play anyway.

In September, Dr. Wier decided exploratory surgery was needed for the growth had become noticeably larger by the week and the pressure was constantly painful, with or without weight.

Surgery was scheduled September 21. Mother was caught in a whirlwind of activity. The day before she had taken Grandma Craig to the Wichita Hospital, where I was to be, for tests. As they arrived at the hospital for my surgery, they received a phone call that Cleah had been taken to St. Francis Hospital for Linda's birth. Dad stayed with me, Mother went to be with Cleah.

The surgeon used a surgical chisel and hammer to knock off the growth from my shin. It came off clean. He sealed the pin-head size hole with plastic, stitched up my leg and ended the ordeal.

Evidently when I hit my leg on the dock, I had made a small hole in the bone. From there grew another bone. The growth was sent to a number of laboratories, including to a bone specialist in Switzerland. They wanted to know how I had grown a bone with complete structure. If they could determine how, they could induce bone growth for those who needed additional bone strength.

As far as I know, mine was a unique incident in nature and not to be duplicated. My leg healed and pictures and information were published in a number of medical journals. My now famous leg didn't garner any money but for the permission for the research, Dr. Wier forgave most of the huge doctor bill.

The week after surgery, Dad left with Aunt Louise and Uncle Wayne to take Grandma and Grandpa Bolton to Jonesboro, Tennessee to visit Grandpa's sister, Aunt Myrtle, and explore the area of his birth and youth.

Mother brought me home from the hospital, still on crutches. The next day she left me home alone to bring Grandma Craig home. Before she returned home that afternoon, our school superintendent, Mr. Kice, brought Raymond home from Dr. Bierman's office with a massive cast on his shoulder. He had been injured practicing football, a sport he should never have tried. He was so small, only 5'2" and 115 pounds.

When Kenneth got home from his football practice, he told me to start dinner and he would take care of the chores. With Dad gone and so much happening he was afraid Mother might have another nerve attack. Fortunately, she took everything in stride. The next day we suggested she go spend the day with Cleah and the baby; they had just come home from the hospital. To our relief, she did.

Within a month, I was off crutches, Raymond was out of his cast, Dad was home, Kenneth was out for football at Friends University and things were back to normal on the farm.

Before basketball season began, Lightner asked me to come to the office for a visit. Reporting had gone so well, he wanted me to put together a reporting system so I could handle all the calls from the 12 schools in the Sedgwick County League. That would mean I'd need five phone calls.

I wrote a letter to all the coaches asking them if they wanted to participate, if so, they should give me a quick call at the school office where Goddard would be playing, make the calls in alphabetical order, keep it brief and I should be able to get my report filed to Lightner in less than 20 minutes after the last game.

The system worked. I started keeping other stats on league play and reported them. I was also the official score keeper for all Goddard games, which put me at the official table. I was not a typical Pep-Club student.

A visiting coach came to give me his line-up and asked if I'd like to join him for dinner after the game. Mr. Kice heard him, informed him I was a student. His reply was, she doesn't look or act the part, why does she have an official position at the table? Mr. Kice said, because she is capable. That boosted my confidence.

It was also the reason I didn't date much in high school. There weren't that many boys and I would not date one of the athletes I needed to cover in my reports. That slimmed the dating field.

Since Kenneth was on the Friends basketball team and I was there, Lightner asked me to start calling in reports of their games. It increased my hours and I started making spending money with my work.

At the fall school program, I had practiced enough

that summer to feel comfortable playing a violin solo, *Adoration*. For the Christmas program I played a medley of Carols. I also sang in the triple trio. Mr. Stiggee was invaluable. He not only taught us American History, he recognized and started teaching us how to study for college courses and tests.

His assignments made us pay attention to world affairs and how they were likely to impact our lives. In 1949 two significant events, the success of the Communists in the China civil war and the Russian detonation of an atomic device redefined the United States' aims to maintain peace in the world. The goal became to contain Communism. We studied the Truman Doctrine and the Marshall Plan. To rebuild the Europe economy, we needed to rebuild Germany as an integral part. To contain China, we needed to rebuild Japan. Both efforts would require continued occupation of troops.

The draft was still in effect and we were keenly aware that the boys in our classes would likely be drafted to participate in the occupation. We also were introduced to a country bordering China, Korea. It was hard to relate to for we were just recovering from fighting a war in Europe, and this little country seemed so unimportant and out of our realm of reference.

Home was where our lives were lived.

Jackye Adams was my friend and school bus companion. Her father was the greens manager for Westlink Golf Course. When I spent the night with her, we went out on the course so she could show me how to play golf. We hit a few balls, then played the first three holes. Coming on to the 3rd hole, I got off a good shot. Then we couldn't find the ball. She was almost teary for it was one of her dad's good balls and she dare not lose it. We searched until I was almost in tears. Finally she looked in the hole and there it was. My first time on the course I had shot a hole-in-one.

In the years to come, neither time nor money afforded me the luxury of learning to play the game. I'd leave that to retirement.

I was also enjoying having Cleah back and sometimes stayed overnight at their apartment to baby-sit with Linda for she was expecting another child in August. One afternoon when I was taking a shower just off their bedroom, thinking Don was not yet home, he was. He walked in, stared at me for several seconds and turned away laughing. I was furious. I did not want to upset Cleah. If I told Mother, she would tell Dad and Don would be in real trouble, the kind Cleah did not need.

I decided then and there not to trust him and stay as far away as possible. I would stop sharing anything of my life with Cleah for she would tell Don and he would make life miserable. He could lie and turn some innocent thing into something it was not.

Spring baseball was opening with the traditional exhibition major league game at Lawrence Stadium. Lightner dropped me a note saying there would be a news conference for famed baseball player Connie Mack and thought it would be good experience for me to attend.

If I could find a way to Wichita, I could ride home from Friends with Kenneth. Mr. Kice told me I could ride in with the grade school kids going to the Orpheum to see "Cinderella." I did, walked the two blocks to the Allis Hotel and Lightner greeted me at the door. He ushered me over to where Mack was sitting, introduced me, told him I wanted an interview and left me standing alone.

Mack invited me to sit with him, told me to go to the bar and get a drink of soda and gin, light on the latter. Drink it slowly, ask for it to be freshened with soda and soon that's all that would be in the glass. My first mixed drink. I was 17 and underage. He told me that too many reporters drank too much free booze at news conferences and wound up with bad interviews. He then asked me more questions than I could ask him. About a half hour later, Lightner came over and asked how I was doing. Mack told him he'd had better interviews but none so delightful and for him to keep me on the staff. Lightner was pleased.

Kenneth picked me up as scheduled. We stopped by so I could give Grandpa a full report. I had done something he had never done, met and visited with one of his heroes. He had played a lot of baseball and was a great fan. I told him I'd told Mack about him and how much time I'd spent at the Courthouse with him. I shall never forget his smile and tear.

Needless to say, but for the record, I did not tell Mother about the soda drink.

I had scholarship offers from Wichita University, Kansas State, the University of Kansas and Oklahoma University. Not unusual for "outstanding senior" students submitted by school superintendents. None were enough to support me and we could not afford to have me go away from home to college. Because of my work at The Eagle and Kenneth already attending, it was decided I could go to Friends University by living at home and riding with him.

I did some special assignment reporting during the summer, the boating regatta at Lake Afton, a few baseball games, nothing major. I stayed in contact with Don Granger but he was called back into the Navy. The mess in Korea, that remote country kept surfacing in the news.

While celebrating Mother's birthday in June 1950, the word came that North Korea had invaded South Korea and Russia was involved. Once again, the United States was taken by surprise. To contain Communism, President Truman responded that if allowed to go unchallenged, it would mean the third world war.

The President first ordered American air and naval forces, then ground troops into battle south of the 38th parallel. General MacArthur, the supremely-egotistical commander, was the tactician. Some believed that to be Truman's first mistake. The war escalated and Mother worried that Kenneth would be drafted since he was a student. He was not. But again, the hot war and the Cold War took a lot of tax dollars and attention.

After living through the massive destruction of WWII, this one seemed like a side note in my life.

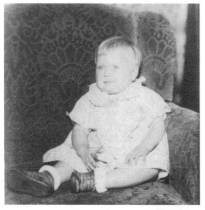

Royal blue eyes won the photo contest.

With Great-Grandmother Craig's home in Wichita, Dad, Mother holding me, Kenneth and Cleah.

During WWII, Mother, Dad, Cleah, me, Raymond and Kenneth.

Taken in 1943, me, Kenneth, Cleah and Raymond in front.

Photos taken in a booth at Woolworth's in 1943 when we moved to the farm.

Eighth grade graduation from Plainview Grade School, one of the last one room schools in the county.

High school sports reporter

Goddard high school basketball team, Chief Jay Hunter, coach. A center, I'm in a different shirt on back row.

Girls trip to Kansas State University in Manhattan.

At 16, walking with Cleah in downtown Wichita.

Senior, boys on either side of me, mixed chorus when I played a violin solo.

With Ron, 9 months.

With Ron on the farm where we lived with my parents.

a. Ron starts school at Alcott Elementary, Christmas picture.
b. Long hair is the high school style.
c. Ron married Kathryn Dettbarn on June 4, 1977; with them are Dick's parents Vincent and Thelma Dilsaver, Poppy, Granny Grace, Dick and me.

Happy day for both, Ron receives PhD from Oklahoma University.

Ron's family, Ron, Kathy, Katie, Kristen and Danny.

The Lazy RB Ranch becomes Ron's.

First to be married grandchild, Kristen and Justin Schmidt wed August 2006. Danny, Katie, Kathy and Ron.

a. & b. Individual pictures at time of engagement.
c. Dick and I married, June 17, 1961.
d. Small wedding, Mother, ill with cancer would attend only with family. With us are Dad, Mother, Cleah, Bob Borlace (Dick's friend, best man), Thelma and Vince Dilsaver.

A happy couple for 43 years of marriage.

a. Our wedding anniversary trip was our first trip to Red River Valley, NM. Second our 10th anniversary. From 1983-2001 an annual trip to Clark family reunion.
b. New England trip, 1977.
c. California, 1972.
d. Atop a camel during '87 trip to Australia to visit Jo and family.

a. One of three trips to London, 1981/1989/1997.

b. A favorite spot to both of us, South Island, New Zealand.

Dick at the Alzheimer's Association Memory Walk in 2003 at the zoo.

Dick's memorial at the Great Plains Nature Center in 2004.

Trip to Colorado, Kensington, KS, 1964 – Debra, Dick, Elmer Lee, Ron, Me.

Christmas 1970 when Elmer Lee came home from Marines/Vietnam, Debra a sophomore, Ron a senior at East High School.

Adults with spouses, Bill and Debra, Dick and me, Elmer Lee, Ron and Kathy

Family grown to include four grandchildren, Ron & Kathy's – Katie, Kristen and Danny; Debra and Bill's - Laura

4. Rapid-fire Lessons

In addition to my work on the sports desk, I was offered afternoon work in the photo department receiving and developing pictures from UPI and AP wire services. I jumped at the chance for it gave me a steady income. Work and school would keep me from baby-sitting. Cleah had a hard delivery and she and the baby were both weak. While she regained her strength, the babies would be at the farm with grandparents for excellent and loving care.

As editor of University Life, I invited both Lightner and Beacon sports editor Bob Donaldson to guest write a column for the paper. In Donaldson's own column in the Beacon, he wrote of the uniqueness of having a girl sports editor of a college newspaper.

That night I was in Dodge City covering the Friends football game. The next morning, much to my surprise, at the top of an unusually lengthy report of the game was my name. My first byline. It didn't get me a raise in pay but certainly a great deal more importance on the job and at school.

Depending upon the week, I worked 25-40 hours a week, carried 16 college hours and was sports editor of University Life. I didn't have time for extra-curricular activities. The school did not have an orchestra so I'd stopped playing the violin except for my own pleasure. I dated some, but work and school took priority. There was no one of particular interest and, as a rule, I did not date those I might need to interview for a story.

The newspaper photographers were always fun. They knew where anything of interest was taking place. If I didn't need to be in the office, I'd tag along. We always stayed out of trouble, but we saw a lot of what was happening in the heart of downtown.

Two of them learned that Elizabeth Taylor and her

new husband, Nicky Hilton, were having breakfast in the dining room at the Lassen Hotel. We ran the two blocks down Market Street, discreetly remained out of sight, to get a glimpse of the not-so-happy couple. We speculated that the marriage wouldn't last long. They were hoping they might have taken the last picture of them together. No such luck, but the two didn't complete the year.

In the summer of 1950, the Ladies Professional Golf Association Tournament (LPGA) was played at Rolling Hills Country Club. The star attraction was the great Elizabeth (Babe) Didrickson Zaharias. I met her the night before tournament play at the news conference. I asked her a question that was later credited to another reporter. I asked her how she loosened up to get such a powerful swing. She told the group she let it all hang loose and swing.

I so badly wanted to go the golf course to watch her in action. All the other sports staff was going. I was left at the desk to cover the afternoon lead stories and file them with the wire service. When the first round was completed, the evening sports writer and great golf expert called to give me the cover and stat story. I had on ear phones and was ready to type. He'd spent too much time at the bar and could not be understood. I got Gene O'Brien, the golf pro on the phone and he gave me the information I needed to write the story along with statistics.

I wrote the story, checked and double checked the notes. Long, the managing editor, came out of his office to check what I had written. He told me it was great, to file it with AP and UPI but to change the byline from mine to Hodge's for he was being paid by them to cover the tournament. Perhaps the best and most important story I had ever written, or event covered, and no credit. Long told me if I was going to play with the big boys to get used to it. Not on your life; I was bitter.

But I had done what no LPGA player did during the

tournament, I had made a hole-in-one on the Westlink Country Club course in the spring before when playing with Jackye.

More lessons were learned out of the classroom than in. The Cleveland Indians were in town for the annual exhibition baseball game. Lightner sent me to the Allis Hotel to get an interview with Bob Feller, the pitching hero. He had left the practice field and the team was headed to the hotel. The evening editor had missed him.

When I arrived the players were all on an upper floor in the hall near their rooms sitting on the floor. Standing and leaning on the hall wall were many briefly dressed females. As I entered the hall I saw Feller at the far end of the hall talking to the team manager, whom I had met at the news conference the day before. One of the players mistook me for one of the "girls."

I wheeled out as fast as I could and nearly ran the block back to the office and told Lightner the situation I'd found and that it was no place to get a professional interview. He finally caught Feller on the phone, laughed with him at the situation and did the interview himself.

In the spring, Lightner gave me the assignment of covering the auto races at CJ Stadium. It was fun because Uncle Gene frequently was with a car crew and I'd take Dad with me. He'd go home with them and I'd pick him up when I finished filing my story. Since college sports had concluded, it provided more hours and income. I not only reported the races, I wrote the advance stories and was paid extra for doing so.

It was not unusual for I was also paid by the column-inch by Friends University for advance stories and pictures that had appeared in The Eagle. That extra income paid for my first year of tuition in college.

In June, there had been no Miss Kansas contest and the professional photographers were making the selection. One of the Eagle photographers was on the selections committee and asked if I could sing. I said yes, but played the violin better. He asked me to submit my name and assured me if I would enter, I would be selected. I told him I was 18 and needed to talk to my parents.

When I told Mother and Dad, she started shaking and yelling at me telling me I would ruin the family name and how immoral it was. Dad finally got her calmed down and said, as you can see, "no."

Later two other photographers had me pose in front of the bar at the Eaton Hotel, which, 50 years earlier, Carry Nation had taken an ax to, breaking the mirror and scarring the wood. I didn't say anything about it, just thought I'd wait for them to see it in the paper. The picture was published for it moved out on wire service but Long decided since I was an Eagle employee, it would not appear in our paper. It did run in the Hutchinson paper and some fellow student's parents clipped it so it was circulated at Friends.

In July 1951, I had my first official vacation and took a Berry Tour with Betty, Jean and Alice, who were friends from West Side Christian Church, to Colorado. We thought we were pretty sophisticated. But since I was not at drinking age, they ordered a beer for me. I stuffed it in my purse as we went from bar to bar in a small Colorado town. It was easier at the Antler's and the Broadmoor. We had whiskey sours with lots of fruit and Jean just ordered a round.

At Eliche's Garden in Denver, we danced with fellows in the crowd to Benny Goodman's orchestra. Dancing to a big band was a new experience for me. The three of them had been to dances at the Blue Moon in Wichita. I had not and I had a ball.

When we were on Grand Lake in a tourist boat, it was hot and I was burning up with the heat. We were floating about and I jumped out of the boat and into the water. It was ice cold. I thought I would drown before they pulled me out. How it could be so hot two feet above water and so cold two feet below was a puzzle I didn't care to test again.

The trip provided new experiences including the very slow train trip home for Kansas was under a major flood. It took us four hours creeping along to go from Hays to Newton. At times the water was up to the floor of the passenger cars and the train was weaving. They told us it was better to keep moving. I had seen high water on the Cowskin Creek and in Wichita on the Arkansas River, but had not traveled through anything like the flood waters of one of Kansas' historic floods.

We learned when we got home that for $5 more for the same length of time, we could have gone to New York City. Betty and I were disappointed, the other two were not.

Back to work, the races and with no air conditioning in the office, it was a very hot, muggy summer. I was to present the Eagle award at the National Baseball Congress tournament. I wore a new brown with white collar sundress to work. It did not go unnoticed on or off the field.

Joe Stone was an Eagle reporter who was in the newsroom that Saturday. His brother Milburn Stone was a film actor in Hollywood and did a lot of screen testing for movie studios. Milburn was in town visiting family. Joe called him to come meet me. He came to the Allis Hotel Copper Oven Cafe for coffee with us. He was impressed, thought I would do well and wanted to schedule a film test the next day.

My picture was in the paper the next morning with comments from both Mother and Dad. I told them about the film test. Again, Mother shook, cried and Dad got her calmed. Nothing more came of the test. I told Joe that my parents objected and I needed to stay in college.

The following day I had an appointment with Dr. Harry Corbin, president of Wichita University. He spent almost two hours with me trying to convince me to come to WU and offered me a good scholarship. Even with it, living costs would be difficult for me to pay and the folks could not.

When I asked him about transferring my hours from Friends to WU, we learned that less than half would. I did not want to start over as a freshman. I thanked him for the compliment and went back to Friends.

There was no degree offered at Friends in journalism, only six hours, so I was majoring in English. The blessing was a wonderful teacher, Mary Greenfield. I came to appreciate really good literature and eventually had 18 hours credit under her. I was still sports editor of the University Life and covered sports for the alumni publication. Football season started and so did a much heavier load at work.

A close college friend of mine was one of the first female jockeys in the bush league of Oklahoma and Kansas. She was riding in Ponca City races. I told Lightner about her and he asked me to go with her for a feature story. The first "feature" with no box score included. We had a great day at the races. Joyce rode well, we got a good picture and the story provided the two of us with "firsts" all our own.

Joyce and I have continued our friendship through the years. We've laughed and cried and prayed and traveled together. The kind of lifelong friendship every person should have to cherish.

Another "first" for me was about to happen.

Mother accompanied me to my first big assignment out of town, the University of Kansas and Kansas State University football game at Lawrence. I had with me a letter of introduction from Lightner addressed to the Publicity Director at KU requesting permission for me to enter the press box. Mother was seated in the stands near by.

As I started to enter, I was stopped. No women were permitted in the press box. I asked for Mr. Pierce; he came immediately. I handed him my credentials. Somewhat shocked at the request, he ushered me to the far end of the facility, much larger than the one at Lawrence Stadium.

The seat I was offered was crowded next to a divider

and the radio reporters were all seated to my left. The man next to me was so large he took up the space for two people. He turned white and I thought he might faint and fall onto my lap. If he did I would go crashing to the floor, smashed and would have to be carried out. The scene was frightening to me and I turned a little white myself.

The situation was not acceptable and I would not be treated so shabbily. I was there as byline reporter from the state's largest newspaper. Since I was accustomed to moving about to talk to other reporters, I did just that. I got out of the seat, with all eyes following me, and proceeded to join those from other newspapers.

Pierce asked everyone covering the game that they not mention me or my presence for he didn't want to call attention to what had just happened: A WOMAN WAS OFFICIALLY IN A UNIVERSITY SPORTS STADIUM PRESS BOX! The forbidden had just happened.

My reaction was, it's a free country; I can go where I please. I continued to visit with others, was offered a seat with the "press" and accepted it. Reporters from the Kansas City Star and Lawrence Daily thought it "a day in history."

Pierce did not find me nor my actions amusing.

At half-time I excused myself, went down to my "assigned" seat with Mother to watch the marching band, bigger and better than anything I'd seen performing live on field. Since I was not doing the stat story, I did not go back to the box until the end of the game. When I did, I caught up with Bill Hodge who was covering the game for The Eagle. He had a good laugh with me, chatted with other writers who all gave me encouragement to be where I needed to be. Hodge from then on turned out to be a real friend.

I wrote a feature story about the big boys playing that Lightner thought was very good and he would try to give me more extra assignments. Hodge had told him I handled myself very well.

Press conferences always provided a lot excitement. If we weren't working, we could all go meet the celebrities who came for one reason or another. I attended as many as I could, but all of the sports celebrities for sure. Ben Hogan was delightful, visited with me and told me I should take up golf, I had a good swing. I had not had a club in my hand!

Although it had been opened for sometime, the Crest Theater was having an opening news conference, hosting a number of movie stars in town for a premier of their western film. Among them was Ward Bond, a sidekick of John Wayne and in most of his films. They'd just finished the movie, "The Quiet Man" and had three more to do. He told me they needed some fresh faces and that my royal blue eyes and beautiful smile would light up the screen. I told him about Milburn Stone a few months earlier. He asked me if I could come to Hollywood, the studio would cover my expenses, for a screen test. He'd call me at the office the next day.

It was late when I got home, woke the folks for I'd be leaving early in the morning to be sure I'd be in the newsroom for the call for we did not have a phone at the farm. When they got the news, Mother had her usual "breakdown." Dad came to the kitchen with me in tears. He said that after all I was 19 years old and could make my own decisions. From then on I was not to ask for their permission but to take responsibility for my own actions. The tears stopped, he hugged me and wished me well.

When Bond called me, I told him I had decided to continue my education and remain working, attending college. He said he understood and that it was probably a good decision.

I felt a little superior about having permission to be on my own. The first time since Red Hen and the strainer that I'd fully felt in control.

As basketball season was beginning, Lightner decided to assign me to cover the Industrial Ice Hockey games at the Alaskan Ice Palace. They would add to my time on the sports desk and give me more byline reporting. I was also still working afternoons in the wire-photo department. They gave me a typewriter so I could write in the lab and go back and forth to the sports desk. I just had to be certain to check the log to get the Weather Map and the Korean War map for the City Editor, Arch O'Bryant. If I missed, I could call and have them repeat it. I was never sure what was showing on the war map that didn't reproduce in print. But O'Bryant always had comments to make when I gave it to him.

O'Bryant was short of reporters and asked me to drive out to the Municipal Airport and try to get an interview with the actor Robert Taylor. He was in getting checked out on his new Beechcraft airplane.

As I passed the coffee shop, there he sat having lunch. I asked if I might join him and he said he would be delighted to have some company. I introduced myself and explained that I usually was on the sports desk but the city editor had asked me to get an interview. He handed me a photo taken by a Beech photographer, a quote that he was looking forward to taking delivery soon for he was leaving for Europe to film a movie.

He left to catch his plane, turned and asked if I'd ever thought of being screen tested – I had a great smile and those royal blue eyes would light up the screen. I said I'd been told that by Ward Bond, but turned him down. He laughed and said, you'll have a happier life.

I came back with more than they thought I could get. O'Bryant told me if they didn't treat me right over on sports, to move to "city" and he could use me. A nice backup offer.

O'Bryant was like a swinging target for the next thing I knew he'd made a real fuss about the first pictures of General Douglas MacArthur when President Truman fired him. He had a voice to carry across the newsroom when he thought reporters were not listening to him. He came thundering in the photo lab yelling at me. At the same time he was throwing a fit, better pictures moved on the wire. It was UPI's fault, not mine. I handed them to him. He recognized what had happened, leaned over and kissed me on the cheek. It helped me recognize that my work with photos and his desk was important to the paper and maybe me.

The old Ford car Kenneth and I had been driving to and from school was shot. Dad said he thought that since I was staying at home and had a paying job, I could afford to buy a used car. He took me to several car lots looking at everything affordable. We settled on an olive green club coup. If he signed the papers, I could borrow the money to pay for it at the State Bank of Colwich and I could make the monthly payments.

When we picked up the car, Dad drove the Ford to Uncle Gene's garage. For a back mechanic bill, Uncle Gene pirated parts except for the rear axle. He and Dad made a two wheel trailer out of what was left.

Kenneth started to work reading meters for the gas company. We shared my car to go to and from Friends. He also drove the folk's car when I had late assignments.

I had gone to the newsroom to help with some desk work before going to the ice hockey game. I got a call from Don Granger; I'd not seen him for he had been called back into the Navy during the Korean Conflict. Good timing, for he had been covering the Stoddard murder case and the two newspapers, The Eagle and The Wichita Beacon, had gotten very nasty with each other in coverage for the Beacon owners, the Levands, were said to have been involved with the girl who was murdered. It's still an open case but Granger's departure was timely.

Granger told me he was getting out of the Navy and would soon be back to work. But, I was the one he needed to talk to about getting copies of the past Korean War maps, put them in an unmarked envelop and give them to his friend. I asked him what it was about and he said he needed them and a friend would pick them up. I had no need to question him further.

His friend would come to the Ice Palace and get them after the game. I took the envelope with me, sat on it at the press table during the hockey game. At intermission, I didn't leave nor did anyone approach me asking for them. After the game, I headed to the car to go to the newsroom to write the story. As I got in the car, the most handsome man I had ever seen stepped between the door and me. He told me he was Granger's friend and asked if I had an envelope for him. I gave it to him and left.

Driving back to the office I had a very strange feeling about what I had just done. I parked the car on the street, went into The Eagle, wrote the story and waited for the proofs to come back up from the press room. I always had to watch it closely and make the usual corrections. The typesetters, especially one, liked it when I used the word "puck" in the story. He'd change the "p" to an "f."

That night I took the proof sheet in to show Long, the managing editor, what the typesetters were doing. Sometime I might not catch it and my byline was at the top. He grabbed the proof and headed downstairs to ream out the entire type-setting crew. It didn't happen again, but it made me later than usual.

Many times after a game I would drop by a nightclub on my way home on West Maple with a proof for some of the players to read. If there were any mistakes, I could call back to the office and get them corrected before press time. Some players were married but came out to unwind after a game. Sometimes it was difficult to tell who was married and who was not.

Tonight was too late. As I walked to the car, my thoughts went back to Granger's friend and I wondered who he was and why he needed the Korea war maps. He had known Granger when he was stationed on Guam.

When I got to the car, he was waiting there. He introduced himself as R. L. Ryan. He had an accent and told me he was from Ireland. I'd just seen "The Quiet Man" three times, so I laughed and said it was nice to meet him. He was about the height of John Wayne but better looking and slimmer. He asked if we could go to the Copper Kettle Cafe, just down the street to have a bite to eat. He had not eaten and was certain I'd not for he'd watched me most of the evening.

I was curious and somewhat drawn to this mutual friend so had no qualms about being with him. As we ate, he asked a lot of questions about me, the paper and the city. How I knew Granger.

He was not forthcoming with much information about himself. He said he was in town at Granger's request to work on a project that was in the talking stage, putting together the Wichita Crime Commission and that they shared other interests. He would be in and out of town for the next two or three months. Could we have dinner again? We certainly could.

For the next month we continued to have dinner at different places, not too public. We frequently ate late at the Allis Hotel. He asked me about going up to a room with him. I told him no, laughed and said I was a virgin and had waited this long, I wasn't going to give in without being married. He asked me to marry him.

To my surprise, I said yes. He made the arrangements and we were to fly to Arkansas the next day where there was no waiting period. Unfortunately I had an ice hockey game to cover so the trip was delayed a day. He had two friends, a man and woman, Jerome and Louise. He said they worked with him and Jerry would be flying the plane. We left, made the round trip during the night. We were married at a small chapel. Ryan took the marriage papers with him for he said he would need them before I would. I knew Mother would find it if I took them home. So I didn't think much about him having them.

I had a full schedule at school, work, being with Ryan as much as time permitted for either of us. I knew Mother would have another "attack" if I told her. If I told Cleah, she would tell Don and I'd have hell to pay for the rest of my life. I did not want him involved. I kept quiet about my friend and my life. After all, Dad had told me to take responsibility for my actions and I was doing just that.

By the time Easter came, Ryan was gone more than he was in town. I wanted a picture of him but he said no, there would be time for that later. I was so busy I didn't have time to waste on what I thought was trivial. Friends' baseball team was doing well, track was in full swing and I had car races starting again. We would have a long weekend in May and he'd be back the last of June. To hurry-up my college schedule, I was taking some summer courses. It always seemed that there would be more time later.

When June came we would talk more about our future. As usual, I went through the cafe, then to the elevator and on to the room the clerk had given me when I called ahead. I got to the room, partially disrobed, an unfortunate event happened. I was shaken but gathered myself together, showered, brushed my hair, freshened my face. And, waited.

Ryan was late getting to the hotel and I was half asleep by the time he arrived. He showered me with hugs and kisses and said we would not have much time. While he was in the bathroom, I picked up his billfold, which was heavy. It had a number of very official badges and cards; he came out before I could read them. When I asked, he simply said he would be back in August, for me to finish classes as soon as I could for he'd like for us to go to Ireland before September. He gave me some cash to help pay for my next semester and spending money.

After the whirlwind but passionate visit, he left in a hurry and I drove home. I was still living at the farm.

The Fourth of July weekend was upon us. Betty, Jean, Alice and I were to go to Sandy Beach for the day. It was difficult not to tell my close friends about Ryan, but he had given me very strict instructions for my safety and his not to say anything until he got back in August.

The Olympics were starting in Helsinki and Lightner and others were going. I would have more desk time to help file their stories when they wired them to us. I was also still in class so the summer passed fast.

Ryan called me at the office as he said he would in August. He was leaving from Portland and would be going back to Guam first. There was an island between Guam and Korea where he might be that was used by the CIA. I knew nothing about them. He probably would be going to Korea from there. When the Republican Convention was concluded, Dwight Eisenhower had quietly gotten the word around that if nominated, he would go to Korea to negotiate peace. Ryan said he needed to be there first.

For my safety, he told me I absolutely was not to mention our phone conversation and certainly nothing about him. He asked me to continue with college, carry a heavy load for a rush to completion, but to please resign from the paper. He absolutely did not want me working in the male environment I was subjected to every day. He did not like some of the sports managers he'd seen coming to the office. Much to my surprise, he knew more about Wichita people than I did and who came to the Sports Desk.

He said he would be back by Thanksgiving and together we would tell my family about our marriage and future plans.

I resigned from The Eagle, telling myself it was time to grow up. But before I did, I arranged with Dr. Watson, Friends' president, to do some public relations work for the university and I was editor of the Talisman, the pictorial year-book for the student body. I would be paid half of whatever ads were sold. Between the two I could manage financially.

I received a package at the university office. In it was cash from Ryan to get me through until he returned. It was postmarked in August from Portland and the office had held it but had not opened it for the president's secretary usually opened all mail addressed to the office. Since it had my name and was marked personal, they finally gave it to me.

I worked in the Life/Talisman office and started scheduling pictures needed for the yearbook. A photographer friend from The Eagle had agreed to take all the pictures for me. Life would be very different but I had made my own choices this time.

In late August, I thought I was just upset with the current events. I did not have my every-two-month period as normal. After several weeks passed, I was painfully aware I was pregnant. I called Granger for lunch and told him, asking how I could contact Ryan. He said he didn't know where he was and wouldn't. Granger was taken by surprise and insisted for my sake and the family that he put an announcement of our marriage in the paper. He went to the library, found a picture and wrote the item.

I had to tell the folks. The three of us were having breakfast for I wanted the light of day for Mother to get the news. Dad said he thought something was going on but would not ask. Mother was so busy taking care of Cleah and her four-children-in-four-years she'd not paid much attention to me.

She cried and apologized that she'd not been more open so I could share more with them. They both assured me that I would stay with them and they would give me whatever support I needed to manage.

Also in October, Eisenhower had announced that he would go to Korea if elected president. I followed the news very closely. Ryan must be in Korea if Eisenhower was headed there.

I looked forward to Thanksgiving and any news. It did not come. Thankfully I was tall, had a number of Pendleton skirts and plaid jackets that kept my condition well concealed. Mother did not mention it to anyone. If Cleah knew, she did not say anything at that time.

A friend of ours died in a very bad snow storm Thanksgiving weekend. He had married and had two children. As I stood with Dad and Kenneth at his graveside, I had the strangest feeling for the first time that it could be Ryan. It really shook me up.

My money was running low. A co-student was working at the Institute of Logopedics and wanted someone to help during the Christmas rush of giving in the Public Relations department. I worked there during the holiday season.

By that time I was well into putting together printing bids, pictures and layouts for the yearbook. I was spending most of my out-of-class time in the Talisman office. And by the end of January, some friends were aware of my condition. I was trying to stay focused, stay in class and keep all things in balance.

The Talisman office was in the lower level at the south end of the building near the main entrance parking. It was icy and for fear of falling, I parked as close as possible.

As I was leaving on a very cold February day, I saw a woman standing next to my car. As I approached I finally recognized it was Louise, Ryan's friend whom I'd only seen on our trip to Arkansas. She smiled, told me to get in the car, and came around to the passenger side.

She told me no one was sorrier than she to deliver the news considering my condition. She said she needed to tell me for she would not be back in the States. Ryan was not coming back. He had been killed when the plane went down in the Korean Sea.

I sat in shock and disbelief. When did it happen, how did it happen, why hadn't someone called me? Thousands of questions ran through my mind.

Jerry had been killed in October under similar circumstances and she was the only one left from the mission. She needed to come see me because it was what Ryan would have wanted.

She told me she needed to leave. There would be no other contact, there was none for me now nor would there be in the future. Ever. Their work had all been undercover and it would remain that way. Ryan had gone to great lengths to protect me. Then she said, you have his child, that's more than she had from Jerry. She said I was a bright woman, nearly finished with college and could raise and enjoy my child knowing that I had been loved enough for someone to risk everything to protect me.

She got out of my car, into hers and left the campus. I sat there crying, shaking, disbelieving what I had just been told. It was too cold to stay long. As I drove home, the reality began to sink in and I had to face telling my family, especially Mother and Dad, what had happened.

Neither Kenneth nor Raymond were home. As Mother and Dad sat with me drinking coffee at the kitchen table I told them what I had just learned. Their response was surprise, but calm. Mother suggested we go to church the next day and make arrangements for a simple memorial service. There was nothing more I could do.

We met with the minister at our church, Westside Christian, planned a ceremony at the end of the Sunday service. There would be a song, a prayer, with flowers at the alter commemorating the life and death of R. L. Ryan. Many friends and relatives attended. It was a fitting closure. It was as our relationship had been – simple, brief, loving.

I will always cherish and return the love he so passionately showered upon me.

5. Love, Loss and Life

Now with support from those about me, I needed to prepare for the arrival of our baby, finish editing the yearbook, catch up with neglected class studies, find a job and get on with my life. But first, I would call Granger for a serious conversation.

I called Granger for lunch at the Copper Kettle Cafe at the Allis. He was happy to meet with me, bought my sandwich, told me the same thing Louise had: nothing more would be forthcoming, no contact to be made. There was no one for me to contact. Ever.

Granger told me I was young and to get on with my life. He thought I should consider coming back to The Eagle but on the news staff. Lightner had called with the same suggestion. If I were to get on with my life, that is not where it would be.

For the next two months, I did what was necessary at school and at home. On March 25th I climbed to the top of the Tower at Friends to finish working with the photographer to take the last of the pictures for the yearbook. As I descended the stairs, I felt a sharp pain and a big kick in my side. I took a deep breath, went to the office to rest for a few minutes, made notes of the pictures we had just taken. I wasn't sure I should drive home, but didn't feel another pain for the next hour. I decided I was safe and went home.

Very early in the morning, I felt another sharp pain. I waited. Three hours later, another came and I awakened the folks. Mother came in to examine me and announced it was time to leave for the hospital. We arrived at St. Francis Hospital a few minutes before 7 a.m. Ronald Raymond Ryan was born on Thursday, March 26, 1953, at 7:30. He weighed 6-pounds, 6-ounces and was 21 inches long. He was a handsome baby with brown hair and eyes.

He was born on Thursday, but the doctor would not let me go home until Monday morning. He told Mother I needed to have some quality time with the baby and to get some rest.

Grandma and Grandpa Craig celebrated their 50th wedding anniversary that Sunday. Grandma Bolton had her 71st birthday on the 28th. She had hoped to finally have a great-grandchild born on her birthday. With their celebrations, they all were happy that I had a healthy child considering the stress I had endured.

It was spring break, so I had a week to relax at home with Ron. Mother had been taking care of Cleah's four children so it would not be a new task for her to care for him. She insisted that she and Dad care for him while I finished school and found a job. I had managed what money I had well but it was running out.

Granger and O'Bryant still wanted me to come back to the paper. A number of friends contacted me, including the managers of the ice hockey teams and Hap Dumont with the National Baseball Congress. Sam Arnholz was most helpful in putting me in contact with John and Ruth Coultis. Ruth was expecting and wanted to be in the office less. They had Coultis Interior Design.

It would be different than anything else I had done, but it was a job with adequate pay and good hours to finish college.

Ruth taught me her bookkeeping and correspondence work as well as how to order fabrics, furniture, and goods from John's design illustrations. It was a different world and I learned so much from them. I had been with the famous, but not with the local wealthy patrons in their business and homes.

Kenneth had graduated, taken a coaching position at Rosalia High School. He and his college sweetheart, Betty Stinle, were married in September. Without him, a major influence throughout my life, everything about me was changing.

I took summer school morning classes before going to work. Miss Crabb, the dean of students, and Cass Riggs, professor of sociology, had a meeting with me. The two of them suggested I change my course of study to sociology after taking a battery of tests. I would need to carry a heavy load my senior year, but they would help me so I could graduate with my class. I carried 17 hours one semester, 18 the other and completed my degree.

When I was 21, I had been married, widowed, had a year-old child, graduated from college and was looking forward to life with Ron.

I finished the year working for John and Ruth, then started looking for career opportunities where I could use my degree to better financial advantage.

Kenneth was drafted into the Army after his first year of teaching. Cleah and Don were moving to Missouri, but since their house had not sold, they stayed at the farm with us for five months while Cleah gave birth to their fifth child.

A number of possibilities gave me some sound choices. I talked to Riggs, Crabb and Granger about each of them. Crabb was an interviewer for Girl Scouts of the U.S.A. They had an opening coming on their staff soon. I accepted an office position, and after two months, was moved to the professional staff as public relations director.

I met with Granger several times while he gave me suggestions of writing news releases, what The Eagle would consider "news" about Girl Scouts and began an 11-year career in what some staff members referred to as the "green veil." Most staff members were single, some stayed that way.

At least Granger was keeping his promise and I had a professional career that would permit new experiences, enhance my resume and advance my carrier for the future.

One of my first assignments, for all staff had them, was directing Day Camp at Camp Seicook (Cookies spelled backward because the sale of cookies by the girls bought the site.) My physical education minor in college helped for I knew something of group activities, and I had two excellent Senior Girl Scouts who knew everything about camping and wanted to prove it. I let them.

By fall the three commercial network television stations in Wichita and Hutchinson were in full production with studios to televise locally. I started Girl Scout programs with each of them. The popular "kid" shows needed kids in the studio every Saturday morning. I sat up a schedule for troop leaders to take Brownie troops and they could include siblings and friends. The only requirement I had was that if they were members, they appear in full uniform.

The Girl Scout uniform was so prevalent, including my wearing it for all television and public appearances, we received a lot of attention. Uniforms also worked for news coverage at both The Eagle and The Beacon as well as still strong radio stations with studio audiences.

Since I needed to be at the stations, I took Ron with me so he could also be seen on TV. We were on a roll. I wanted to move to Wichita and get a baby-sitter for him. This time it was Dad who insisted I stay put and let Ron be with him; he needed a man's discipline. It worked. Ron and I continued to live at the farm.

At one time I had three television shows at each of the three stations on the same day. It kept me moving and gave me a lot of exposure in the community.

The medium was not only new for me, it was for others and the first live telecast of national Democrat and Republican conventions were carried nationally. It would also be the first presidential election in which I could vote.

All our family were Democrats and I hadn't gotten

over Eisenhower's Korean trip. I thought he could have handled it differently and my life would have been different. So, I did not vote for the second term for Eisenhower, I voted for a very bright man and excellent writer, Adlai Stevenson.

The Cold War was in full progress with Russia. Senator Eugene McCarthy was still on his hunt for communists, terrorizing anyone who had a persuasion toward socialism in this country. We had bomb shelters, every neighborhood had a Civil Defense group and the news was full of Russian advances into other countries, including Czechoslovakia, again.

Life on the farm and life in Kansas remained much the same. Private aviation and military contracts kept the labor market strong. McConnell Air Force Base had opened, adding military to the community mix and many more flights overhead.

The Big Ditch flood project that Grandpa Craig had fought so hard to build three bridges was progressing, but with only two bridges and a cockeyed arrangement at 13th and 21st streets. Granger was covering much of what was happening during construction and kept in close contact with Grandpa.

Wichita was being kind to me and my work was going well. I did not date, nor was I interested. I joined Wichita Press Women, a journalism professional organization, was becoming involved in the United Way and was still an active member of Westside Christian Church where I sang in the choir.

The Girl Scout national organization insisted that all professional staff members have a month of training by national staff members. I was no exception. Betsy Long, Dick Long's daughter, and I would attend a month of training in April. It was hard to be gone but Mother and Ron drew pictures and sent me many letters.

We were at Mammoth Cave, near Bowling Green,

Kentucky. The national staff did not want to do the radio, newspaper, or television interviews. They sent me to town to do all of them. For a week I was making public appearances more than I was in training. We didn't have to wear our uniform unless we were in public. I wore it almost daily while others relaxed in jeans.

We had fun collectively writing a show for the closing night's program. I'd been keeping notes throughout the month and we had some great lines, producing a very funny show.

The Kentucky Derby was being run the day after training ended. We were given permission on our liberty weekend to go to Louisville to check out where we could park, the best way in and out of town and see part of the state besides the caves and hotel on the landing. We were set. The hotel gave us permission to stay over, and we left early in the morning with a box breakfast.

We had left it to Martha to get the tickets. We thought she had gotten them up in the stands where we would be seated as ladies to watch the grand race. Boy, were we surprised. Betsy and I were dressed to the nines in heels and hose and fashionable dresses. Our tickets were out in the paddock. We arrived in time to tour the barns, visit with some of the jockeys, get a close look at the horses. Then off to the inside field we went. Thankfully it was dry.

We felt ridiculous surrounded by people in jeans and work clothes. I swore that if I ever attended again, I'd get my own ticket and wear the biggest, most glamorous hat I could find so I could sit and sip a mint julep as is meant to be. Maybe someday I'll do that.

The exposure and recommendation from the national staff prompted a contact from the nation Public Relations Department about the position of Radio Manager on the national staff. It would mean moving to New York City and the job did not pay enough for me and Ron to live there. I turned it down. I was content with my work and recognition in Wichita.

It was the right decision for Ron was developing well, a fun, laughing child with eyes as bright as his mind. Raymond spent a lot of time with him playing games. For his birthday, the folks gave him two lambs, Spring and Jupiter. He started feeding them with a bottle and had chore responsibilities. I bought him a miniature Allis Chalmers tractor and trailer for him to "haul" feed to them and to keep him from climbing onto Dad's big tractor. He was doing well.

Since there was a lot of public relations activity taking place at McConnell Air Force Base and Olive Ann Beech was a major sponsor of the Senior "Wing" Girl Scouts, I was assigned District Director, which encompassed it. The assignment did add a bit of color to my routine life.

General and Mary Coddington, the base commander and wife, lived on the base. Mary was very active and would be the Neighborhood Chairman of the Girl Scouts on base. She called me to come to her home to meet her and go over her organization and schedule.

When we sat down to coffee, she had every position filled with leaders. Colonels' and Majors' wives would assist her. Captains' and Lieutenants' wives would be troop leaders, NCO wives would be assistants, others would be troop committee members. All I could do was smile at her and say, I'm sure it will work.

Our Executive Director, Jayne Smith, was anxious to know how my meeting went, replied that it was a volunteer organization and to stay on top of the situation.

That gave me reason to spend more time with Major and Dottie Tacker, the Public Information Officer there. I became acquainted with a number of the single officers and the Tackers invited me to join them at the Officer's Club for many parties. I dated one several times, but he was from Chicago, not here for long, and the budding romance did not go far for I was not moving.

At one of the Brownie father-daughter banquets where I was to be the speaker, a Captain came up to me and said he was a Girl Scout volunteer. I asked, "What position?" He said, a Girl Scout leader breeder. I burst out laughing.

As I was speaking about the World Organization of Girl Scouts and Girl Guides and opportunities for their daughters wherever they were stationed, I kept getting a glimpse of him smiling at me. One of the most difficult public speeches I ever made.

On Air Force Day, I completed setting up the Wing Scout display in the public hangar and was due to be on the reviewing stand with dignitaries. When I was midway between the stand and the hangar, the Air Force Thunderbird Jet Team came in low over the runway. With them right above me, alone on the wide stretch of concrete, I ducked. The AF photographer caught it straight on, me and the planes.

Tacker had the photo plastered all over the PIO office from several military publications. From it and meetings, many on base knew me. As I drove onto base the guards would wave me on in; some thought I was a Marine officer because of the green dress uniform.

Mary had set up an early morning meeting so I needed to be on base almost at the crack of dawn. I was waved on, got to her house for coffee and to go over her agenda. Suddenly the General burst into the breakfast area, yelling, "What the hell are you doing here?"

At the time, McConnell was part of the Strategic Air Command and the security squad had just arrived for inspection. The base was on lock-down. No one could come on or leave the base.

The General told me to make one call fast and plan to spend the night on base. I called the office quickly, told them I was on base and would be back tomorrow. Most of those we needed at the meeting lived on base and we had plenty of time to put together the full schedule for the Girl Scouts for the rest of the year.

I learned a lot about military wives from Mary. She was a major support and guide to wives of her husband's staff. They were a tight-knit group raising their children, not seeing much of their husbands and ever so dedicated to their husband's careers.

Before they left Wichita, I saw to it that Mary was nominated for and received the highest award given a Girl Scout volunteer, the Girl Scout Thanks Badge. It was also at McConnell AFB that Coddington himself received a major promotion – to General. They liked Wichita.

A wide variety of activities needed attention – traditional events, summer camping, cookie sales, the annual Girl Scout Doll and Toy Festival, international events and troop activities – which put me in constant contact with news editors and reporters.

After two years on the staff, I was selected as a staff member to attend the National Girl Scout Convention in Philadelphia, which included the pre-professional staff conference. A first for me.

Since I would be in uniform most of the time, I purchased a very nice black coat with a white mink collar and a nearly matching white fur hat. We used the steps on and off the plane.

As I stepped onto the platform, a sea of Senior Girl Scouts near the terminal started yelling and screaming, "Grace, Grace, there she is." Grace Kelly was due to arrive in town and the girls mistakenly took me to be her. As I got to the bottom of the step, a guard took my arm, ushered me to a side door, asked my name and where I was staying. He would see to it that I got my luggage but please get in the cab and go so he could get rid of all those kids.

I did just that. When I was checking in to the hotel, of course, I had no luggage. A crowd of girls started yelling,

"She's here!" This time it was not for Grace Kelly, but they had heard the actress, Donna Reed, was staying at the hotel and was in a play next door. With my fur hat still in place, I got my room key, and since my name was Donna Ryan, that's how I signed their programs.

The two women look nothing alike; how could I possibly have been mistaken for both within the past hour? But it was flattering.

Between the two national meetings, five of us decided we wanted to see New York City for the first time. One of the girl's boyfriends had taken his MD internship there and mapped out an all night tour for us. We took the five o'clock train, went to the Statue of Liberty, the Empire State Building, the United Nations, had dinner at a great small Italian restaurant, rode a Hansom in Central Park, went to the Waldorf Astoria for a cocktail, toured Broadway, walked the streets, rode in cabs, rode the subway and returned to Philly in time for some to go to 6 a.m. mass.

Jayne, who was from New York, could not believe all we had done in such a short time – a week's tour in less than 12 hours.

From there I went to spend the weekend in Washington, D.C., with the Tackers. Larry was now stationed at the Pentagon. I stayed at the Willard Hotel and took two day tours, saw a play, "A Country Wife," and spent Sunday at the Tackers' home. Monday I flew to Tulsa, saw Jean Stiles, then flew home to be in the office Tuesday morning. It had been an exhilarating experience and I learned more in a week than I had been exposed to in a lifetime of minimum travel. Mainly, I learned I could do just fine traveling by myself.

During most of the '50s there was much hype about the space program and how one nation one day could blow-up the other from far distances. It wasn't until the Russians put up a space capsule with a dog named Sputnik that the world took notice of its importance.

Ron named his dog Sputnik and the two of them jumped off hay bales pretending to be in outer space. The farm offered that kind of play and dreaming for him.

Many of Eisenhower's civil rights, cross-country highway development and extension of natural gas developments changed much of the country. Cars became the major transportation leaving train service sitting on the rails. Oil field development permitted plentiful fuel for cars, trucks and airplanes to set the nation in major economic development. Internationally the Cold War raged on with the Russian Soviet Union expansion a threat to world order and peace.

At home, in schools, in churches and organizations, life was good. Television, not movies brought news into living rooms morning, noon and night from around the world. Anyone interested in being informed could do so in the new electronic age.

Staff member Dolores Collins' father was a leader in the Democrat Party and was hosting Eleanor Roosevelt, in town for the Little United Nations dinner. He made arrangements for Dolores and me to have afternoon tea with Mrs. Roosevelt. We arrived at the hotel in full uniform, nervous.

We were greeted by her secretary and ushered into a sitting room where she had been taking a nap. She sat up, wiped her face with a kerchief, smiled and complimented us on our appearance. For the next half hour she drilled us on how we could tie in the World Association of Girl Scouts and Girl Guides with the United Nations.

We were there for tea, not to reorganize the national organization or make any commitments. We told her we thought there could be many areas of cooperation and we would offer the national staff our report.

When we told Jayne about it back at the office, she nearly blew her top. But we sent off a report to the national PR staff and asked them to contact Mrs. Roosevelt's office. We moved the ball off of our court as fast as possible.

That fall, we had another encounter with a prestigious politician. President Harry Truman.

We were in Kansas City, Missouri, for our regional professional staff meeting. As part of the program, we were to tour the Truman Library in Independence. As we approached the reception area, we were asked to step into line to meet Mr. Truman. Several of the staff were ahead of us, then came Dagmar, the tallest, then Mary, near my height, then me. As Mr. Truman looked up at us, he started singing, "Oh the girls they grow tall in Kansas…The girls they grow tall and the boys love 'em all."

I was standing in front of him at that point, and he reached out to give me a big bear hug. Mary gave him a very strange glance over her shoulder. Later she teased me about being hugged by the President of the United States. What a thrill. His face came into my chest.

In Wichita, a group of Public Relations professionals in the city had been working to put together a local committee to form the foundation necessary to establish a local chapter of Public Relations Society of America (PRSA) in Kansas. Several people from throughout the state started having joint meetings. A conference was scheduled in Lawrence. I was invited to attend and the council would cover my expenses.

Since I was the only woman attending from Wichita, the fellows from here were very gracious and escorted me to receptions and dinners. They may even have had designated events for there always seemed to be an escort at the right place at the right time.

Bill Walker, a good friend from Vickers Petroleum Company, escorted me to the closing reception and dinner. I had purchased a red and white silk print dress with a matching red linen hem-length coat, the most attractive outfit I had ever had. I had many compliments from all my escorts. One was exceptional.

A man walked up behind me, said in my ear, "Damn but you are fetching."

Bill smiled and said maybe he should introduce us with a line like that. I turned and there was a smiling, nice looking man, to whom Bill turned and said, "Donna, meet one of the brightest among us. Dick Dilsaver, PR director of the Menninger Foundation and president of the Topeka group."

He then asked Dick if he would provide me with a list of speakers he had compiled and to see if we could get any of them to come speak in Wichita.

After the banquet, many adjourned to the hotel suite of Gertrude Lewis, PR for the Atchison, Topeka, and Santa Fe railroads, and Jane Dennery, PR for Blue Cross Blue Shield. Since liquor by the drink was prohibited in Kansas, those two set up a hospitality bar in their suite and held forth royally. I knew both of them from Kansas Press Women, and they graciously invited me to join their party.

After a few drinks, Dick Hunter started teasing Jane about her "crush" now being available. He'd moved into an apartment in Topeka.

Jane was blushing and it dawned on me that Hunter was talking about Dick Dilsaver. The fellow with the compliment I'd just met. I smiled at Jane when I made the connection.

The next week there arrived at the office a list of excellent speakers to fill my year's calendar with programs.

Walker and I went to lunch to talk about the schedule of speakers and discuss a possible Girl Scout project at Cowtown, a museum being built on the Arkansas River to salvage historic buildings of the city.

He complimented me on the programs arranged for the Wichita Public Relations Society and asked me if I had heard that Dilsaver had left Menninger's and was taking on Press Secretary for Clyde Reed, sure to be the next governor of Kansas. He then said he thought Dilsaver could accomplish a lot if he could focus on what he wanted to do, politics, write, for he was one of the best, or go back to the newspaper business.

We continued our discussion of the Girl Scout project. I told him we could not raise funds but we might be in a position to help as guides on the site. He got a little carried away and wanted the girls in period dresses. I said no, to introduce a program, the girls would need to be in uniform. Good. He would call Dick Long at the paper who was chairman of the project and have him write a letter to the Girl Scouts board of directors.

The letter followed, the board accepted and board member Marge Kirby volunteered to be the site director. From that started the guide program of national recognition, in which literally thousands of girls participated and would continue to celebrate its 50th Anniversary.

In August, the National Baseball Congress was beginning the national tournament and to have a crowd for the Mutual Game of the Day national broadcast, they declared it Boy Scout and Girl Scout Day. They could get in free along with their drivers.

I was in the Press Box at Lawrence Stadium to do the color segment at the seventh inning along with a Boy Scout staff member. After being seated, much to my surprise, in walked Bob Feller. I did not remind him of my first encounter with him at the Allis Hotel when I was a newspaper sports reporter.

Gene Elston was doing the play-by-play broadcast. When it came our turn, the Boy Scout answered with only yes or no. Feller could not get him to talk. He turned to me and I started giving him our "national" story, which included activities that summer in a number of states. Feller got up, leaned against the wall and left me chatting to his national audience, laughing. Elston came back, pushed him to the chair and we wound up one of the longest periods I was on national radio.

Feller was impressed and asked if I could come to Minneapolis to the World Series to do some similar color with him. It would be a first – no other woman had ever been officially on Mutual's Game of the Day.

When I went back to the office, they had been listening to me on the radio and thought I did superbly. I told Jayne about my offer and thought it would be good for GSU-SA. She did not. She told me if I wanted to trek off to flatter myself more, go, but I would not be in the Council's employment any longer.

I could not afford to leave my position for a one-show appearance. On my way home, I picked up Feller and Elston to take them to the airport. They could not believe I could not do a couple of shows. Then Elston told me he did not know if Feller had the authority to make those arrangements without management approval. I'll never know what might have happened in my career had I taken the risk. I saw Elston in Wichita the next year as they closed off the radio show. He then became the voice of the Houston Astro baseball team.

My workload was heavy and I needed to start Ron in kindergarten. Our offices were now on East Central and the drive to and from work was taking a lot of time. I started checking on schools and wanted him to attend one of the top public schools recommended by teachers. I began looking for a house to buy near Alcott School and found one two blocks away.

Raymond was coming home from the Army and would be back home. Two years before he left he had given me a check to pay for wheat seed because we were in the midst of a two-year draught. He would keep the folks occupied and be there to help Dad with the farm at Norwich. His money had saved the farm during the draught of '55 and

'56.

When I signed for the loan to purchase the house, they learned I was a single woman. I could not qualify unless a man co-signed the note. The folks agreed and Dad signed with me. If I could have paid for the house, I could have purchased it out right, but needing a loan I didn't have a choice. I wanted to do it on my own, but could not.

Ron and I moved to our first home, 3602 Oneida. A red brick, two bedroom, full basement, attached garage with a spacious back yard. It was just right for us. It was hard on both Mother and Dad, but with Raymond home from the Army to keep them company and watch evening TV it worked. Frequently they came in after school on Friday to pick Ron up for the weekend.

He was adjusting to kindergarten and being in the city with neighborhood friends. Being closer to work gave me much more time with him. I did not date but kept busy with home, work and social activities in the community.

My television responsibilities grew as more live variety shows were introduced. Ethel Jane King had a noon show on KAKE TV and whenever she needed a guest by noon, she would call me for an appearance on a moment's notice. There were like shows on the other two stations, giving me almost weekly appearances.

Radio broadcasts gave us an opportunity to reach a larger segment of the population who were only beginning to acquire television sets in the rural and lower income areas of the city.

President Eisenhower would be going out of office and the political races were heating up. Richard Nixon was sure he would be the Republican candidate, but I never did care for him. Lyndon Johnson was certain to be the Democrat choice.

A young senator from Massachusetts, John F. Kennedy, was coming on strong and coming to Wichita for a brief lunch visit. He was to be downtown at Bulls and Bears, across from the Lassen Hotel. I was at a United Way meeting and watched him come out to the street. If looks would get the nomination, he had it cinched. He was young, energetic, and wanted to get the country moving. He did not say where he wanted to move it to.

At a United Way meeting, it was decided that because of all the work I had done on the PR committee, I should go to the National UW Convention in St. Louis, Missouri. I had visited there many times for Cleah and family lived south of there at Crystal City. This trip was different. I roomed with Assistant Executive Director Margo Ray. She and the fellows attending knew how to party. We didn't miss a session of the meeting nor any of the jazz groups in town. The convention put me on a different level with community leaders than I had been at home.

Walker and I had lunch many times to plan coverage for the Cowtown program and activities for PRSA. I worked with Granger to get a couple of major photo-spreads for both GS camps and the Cowtown guide program, which was going very well. It was one of the best community relations projects ever undertaken by the Council.

He also told me that Dick Dilsaver was back in town from the University of Richmond where he had been doing some fundraising. He said he would be a good addition for our PR group and to invite him to the next meeting if I happened to get a call from him. Paul Dannelley was helping him find a suitable position here. They both said Dick was overqualified for most openings they knew about but that he wanted to be back in Kansas and closer to his two kids in Topeka. I did not hear from him until a surprise call at home.

One Friday evening, Ron wanted to go to a movie. I told him I wanted to get the laundry out of the way and I was already in jeans and a sweatshirt. I heard the phone ring. Ron answered. When I came upstairs, I asked who had called; he said it was a business asset of mine and he was coming to go to the movie with us.

Not knowing who my "asset" was, I dashed to change clothes and brush my hair. I answered the door, and there stood Dick Dilsaver. He had a packet of information for me, and we went to a movie.

The three of us began going out to dinner, the movies and Joyland on a regular basis. Ron, Dick and I began dating.

6. A New Career – Electrically

The political campaign was heating up and so was my relationship with Dick. He was good with Ron, the most important element in our continued relationship, and was working in real estate for a good company. His co-workers liked him and started inviting us as a couple to theater, shows and concerts. It was nice to be a couple.

Kennedy was elected President and there was an air of newness in so many facets of local, state and federal government. The space program was moving into major importance and was introducing many new products including the giant computers starting to run much of business. Everything seemed upbeat at work, home and the atmosphere in the country.

Then a major blow came. Mother was diagnosed with cancer in April. It was advanced but they did many surgeries trying to stay ahead of the spread. I spent so much time with her in the hospital. I could not believe that she was not to be with us much longer. She was showing so much courage, faith and love she became a strength for all of us.

She asked so many questions about Dick. As I answered them, I became even more aware of how much I had fallen in love with this highly intelligent, gentle, patient, understanding and kind man.

She wanted Dick and I to proceed with our wedding plans in June. She would attend if we had only a small ceremony with immediate family. I bought a dress for her that would cover the bladder elimination bag attached to her stomach. It was not evident. Her best month was June into July.

On June 17, 1961, Dick and I were married at Westside Christian Church. Later as I looked at the pictures I became aware of what a sacrifice she had made to be there.

We returned from our two week wedding trip and I realized the cancer was back. The first week in August after a colonoscopy, they gave her maybe two weeks to live. Dad began taking care of her. Ron and I were at the farm every night and I did not have to give Girl Scout training.

In October, December and February when she was hospitalized, Dad asked Cleah to come stay a week and help him care for her.

I juggled everything – work, home, a new husband who was so generous, understanding and gracious about my time spent with Mother. Because of Dad's superb care, she made it through Thanksgiving, then Christmas, then Valentine's Day, all in very heavy snowy, winter weather.

She said she did not want her family, especially her grandchildren, to stand at her grave on the ice and think of her being placed in a snow covered grave. The last of February, that Sunday afternoon, while sitting on the edge of the bed, she saw a robin perched in the tree outside her window. She looked at me, smiled, and said, spring is here.

On Friday night, March 2nd, Dick went with us to spend the night at the farm. I visited with her last about 10:30 and she sent me to bed. Dick stayed with her until she slipped into a coma. We called the ambulance after lunch to take her to St. Francis Hospital.

Raymond and Dad went for coffee while they connected the IV. Reverend Hill was with me in the room when she died at 3:15, March 3, 1962. She was the first person I had ever seen pass away, and could honestly let go and say to myself, "Let her go to be with God. She deserves to be without pain and have some rest."

The next few weeks of adjustment were very difficult but I had a lot of work to get done. The Girl Scouts had written all new programs and added a level; there would now be Brownies, Junior, Cadette and Senior Girl Scouts. We had a lot of training to do.

I made arrangements with KAKE TV manager Martin Umansky to have a half hour each Saturday morning for four weeks of television training, one program session on each of the new programs. We were the only Council in the nation to pull together the massive training program on television.

I wrote, directed and produced the shows using approved Girl Scout material and the new books. Leaders from across the state tuned in and gave the station the largest Saturday morning ratings they had ever had.

Upon completing the training project, we had only weeks to develop the celebration for the 50th Anniversary of GSUSA. Working with friends at Wichita State University athletics department, we planned the half-time ceremony for the opening football game. I organized and then directed a 1,000 girl chorus seated on bleachers near the end-field. We had a parade of flags with a girl on each 5-yard line on each side of the field. A Brownie in a new Cadillac convertible was driven in to represent all the girls in the stands. Parents and drivers were admitted free of charge and sat in the seats of the not-yet-organized marching band.

It was the largest crowd ever assembled for a WSU football game at that time. The university was happy because of all the coverage TV and newspapers gave the event. Almost more than the game itself.

We then had a visit from Lady Baden Powell whose husband was the founder of the Boy Scouts. We had a luncheon for her at Innes Tea Room, followed by a tree planting ceremony at the GS Little House. It was best not to move her to too many locations, so I called a news conference there at the little house in Sim Park. She sat in front of the fireplace and was so happy to be on television; all the stations, newspaper and a couple of radio stations covered her visit.

She told me she would like to have me travel to make more arrangements for she wanted the organization to have more recognition with little effort on her part. She was charming. My time and picture with her, which I cannot locate, was a highlight of my GS staff time.

During the months that followed, Charlie Pearson, one of Dick's KU journalism professors, talked him to coming to The Eagle, "where he belonged." It was a good move, but because of my work we needed to have some arrangement for Dick not to be involved in any way with my contacts at the newspaper.

Because of Dick's newspaper work, we were invited to the Kansas Chamber of Commerce State Meeting at the Lassen Hotel. As Dick circled the room chatting with many people he knew from across the state, I noticed a man standing aside surveying the crowd.

I went over to him and said, welcome to Wichita. Do you know many people here? Not many here from Wichita. I began walking with him around the ballroom giving him names of business leaders and their companies, or organizations. After the tour, we separated and I caught up with Dick.

I then saw the man going up to people, calling them by name and asking about their business by name and shaking hands with his left hand. I was fascinated and asked Dick who he was. He said, that's Representative Robert Dole. You'll be hearing a lot more about him when he runs for the Senate. An event to remember.

In November, at the Girl Scout Doll and Toy Festival we were in the process of displaying at the Wichita Forum, the large civic building downtown, Dolores came in saying, "Have you heard the news? I've just been told to turn on the radio. President Kennedy has been shot in Dallas."

We joined the nation in shock. We also needed to know what to do about the program with hundreds of families coming for the Brownie Christmas Sing that night. I called Jayne, but was told she was so shattered she could not talk on the phone. I tried to get into the newsrooms at radio and TV stations to cancel the Sing. No line possible.

With the stage set with a large Christmas tree with huge streamers going to oversized candles, the music director and I decided to proceed with the Sing. That night families poured into the balcony seats to capacity. I told Myrth Klobescher to put on her white gloves; she resisted and I insisted. I pulled down the house lights, her white gloves shown up for direction to the girls, pulled up lights on the tree and candles. The Brownies began singing, filling the massive hall with angelic voices.

I had Myrth hold for the last song, "Silent Night," and had her announce that this song would be in tribute to the President. As the small voices filled the giant space, I dimmed the tree lights and left the lights on the candles. There was not a dry eye in the house, including mine.

Going into Christmas, I received one of the most complimentary letters of my career. It was from an Air Force Colonel who thanked us for keeping faith and not making the day morbid for the children in attendance at the Sing. We gave them something to do that would remain with them the rest of their lives. They would remember the day the President was shot and the song they sang for him. I still hear from girls, now adults who talk about where they were and what they did on November 22, 1963. All have good memories.

In the spring, Dad married a woman he'd known years before, and Grace Rutledge Snyder became my stepmother. It was good for Dad for they started having a life together and not depending so much on me. Raymond was married to Phyllis and had two small children and frequent visitors. I seemed to become their surrogate grandmother. The family was changing and so was the country.

Lyndon Johnson's administration was introducing more new programs so social services were expanding nationally, state and locally. Some offices were being set up but not staffed or directed. And he was building up the Defense Department and escalating the war in Vietnam, a country most of us had never heard of but if the Communists were about to take over, we would follow the policy to stop the expansion.

Integration was a slow process, Brown vs. the Topeka School Board got international attention and all of society changed, not knowing what would happen next or who to trust.

Ron and Dick were doing well at school and work. Ron still spent a lot of time with Dad at the farm and in the small town of Norwich where he and Grace now lived.

In the summer of 1965, Dick announced to me that his son, Elmer Lee, would be coming to live with us to go to East High School. He and his stepfather were not getting along well and he needed to be in a bigger school for a better education.

I began looking for a larger house for the one I owned was not large enough to accommodate the growing family and growing boys. I found one that needed some remodeling just up the block that had 2 acres of land and a room for each boy, a den for Dick, a main-floor laundry room for me, family, dining and living rooms with a two-car garage and upstairs apartment. We bought it and I sold the little house.

The remodeling project had to be done while I would be gone for a month. Not good timing.

The National Girl Scout Round-up was to be held in July in Idaho and I was to be on the national public relations staff as magazine director. I would be driving with the Council president, which would take more time for she needed to be on site a week early.

Dick and Dad worked with me to cover all the month's schedule for Ron including a week at Boy Scout camp. It took a lot of cooperation and understanding from them to make it possible for me to be away.

We arrived at the Round-up site at Coeur d'Alene, Idaho, on schedule for Mary Ellen but too early for me to check-in so I drove on to Washington to visit Dick's Aunt Grace. On the way, I took a wrong turn at a detour and wound up at the guard gate of the Atomic Energy Reservation. It took many phone calls back to Wichita to have the guard release me and Mary Ellen's car. By the time I was driving away, there were another half-dozen cars with families who had done the same thing. That was my first visit to the reservation. I'm lucky I was not jailed.

The 10,000 girls attending the Round-up from the USA and around the world made a magnificent sight in the amphitheater at night offering many photo ops for magazines of all topics.

When we received word that Adlai Stephenson had died and the flags were to be lowered to half-staff, the national office had to contact every country's embassy of every flag represented to do that. Life magazine called wanting a photo of the flags. We finally got them, packaged them and drove them to the airport at Spokane. All that work and they did not use them, but they were some of the best photos I ever arranged.

We had a steady stream of VIPs coming through the PR reception area. I was told that Idaho's Senator Frank Church was on his way. I dashed out of the tent into my office so as not to have to escort him around the site. I ran into him literally head-on. Since I was injured I didn't need to go. He said he was sorry, patted me on the shoulder and said he would very much have enjoyed me being his escort. The staff never stopped teasing me.

As we were closing shop, the PR director asked me if I would consider coming to New York on the national staff to handle what I'd established with magazines at the Round-up. That one was an easy turn-down but it started me thinking about what else I might be capable of doing in my career.

Upon arriving home, we finished the house project and had to rush the move for Elmer's things had been deposited in the garage of the house where we were moving. Lock, stock and stuff. I took a week to get the house organized, new furniture in place, clothing stored and, thankfully, a very large back porch with wall-to-wall cabinets for extra coats, balls, bats, you name it. Dick's Dad came to help with some tree trimming and thought it quite an "estate."

Elmer Lee started East High and the football team. Ron joined some of his elementary friends for intermediate school at Roosevelt. We would manage.

Dick's work at The Eagle was going well and we were being invited to many social events, some because of his position, some because of mine. One was the Emerald Ball sponsored by a hospital and always had a "star" attending. That year it was Robert Young of film and TV fame.

He asked me to dance with him and it felt like I had 10 feet. He was easy to slide with but I also noticed how almost robotic he was, then it dawned on me, the man has really been drinking. He left the ball early. It was fun to know I could keep up and not be embarrassed if asked to dance again. Dick's football-injured knee didn't let him enjoy dancing. It gave out on him once on the dance floor and I had to almost carry him off. Seldom again did we try.

In a couple of months, May 1966, came the Wichita Press Women's Beaux Arts Ball–a costume/theme event. I was chairman with a great committee. It was our scholarship fundraiser and we had excellent participation from TV stations, newspapers, advertising agencies and other organizations all giving us major news coverage.

I talked the couples of the Girl Scout staff to join my group. They'd come if they did not have to wear costumes. So, we decided on the theme from the movie, "A Ship of Fools." Dick was captain. It was fun with many compliments on the success.

Although I had heard much of his childhood friend, Kent Carroll, almost from the day I met Dick, he didn't talk a lot about him until that night. Being in a navy jacket may have spurred him on. It wasn't until then that I knew how deeply he felt for his friend and how much he missed him. He was one of a few he stayed in contact with through personal letters at Christmas.

That was not the only enlightenment that came from that night. It was not until I saw the pictures that I realized while I had been the Belle of the Ball, Dick had been drinking. It had been a problem the first year of our marriage but not since. He had stopped with counseling. That was the slow beginning of a later roller-coaster ride for the family. Sometimes I was too busy with work to notice the growing problem.

I had been among the first to be loaned to the United Way as a Loaned Executive, to do some work in the public relations office to kickoff the campaign. An artist friend helped me design four large visual thermometers so TV and the newspaper could use them to report the goals reached. They were a big success that came with a lot of credit to me from the staff.

In the next year our staff was diminishing in size, adding more work to those of us still on staff. There were positions open but the ED was not recruiting nor interviewing for staff replacement. We were all exhausted.

Then came a call from Bob Rives at KG&E asking if Fred Kimball, his VP, could turn my name in to the search committee for the Wichita State University public information manager position. I gave my consent and had several interviews with Dean Duerkson, search chairman. At the end of the month, I was one of three candidates and the only woman still being considered. I was impressed.

Then Rives called, saying Kimball asked if I would

interview with WSU, would I consider interviewing for a position he was thinking about creating at KG&E? I said I would talk to anyone.

Several interviews were arranged. First with Marketing VP Bill Byrne. Then Norman Jacobshagen, the advertising manager, was included. At the end of the third interview, Byrne leaned back in his chair, put his feet on the desk and asked what made me think I could handle the job they were thinking about.

I told him I would not have wasted his time or mine in these interviews if I didn't think I could do whatever it was they wanted done in marketing/public relations. He said, I like your vinegar. We agreed, I would start to work on January 3, 1967, with a substantial increase in salary.

I resigned my position with the Girl Scouts to begin a 25-year career with KG&E. I was the first woman hired in a non-traditional position by the utility. I learned much later that I was one of a handful in the nation. They had traditional office workers and Home Economists, but no other professional staff women. I was the only woman with a male counterpart for salary consideration.

I was exempt from overtime, had a private office, shared a secretary and had an expense account for travel. I had all but the latter with the Girl Scouts, so knew exactly what to request.

On Tuesday, following New Year's weekend January 3, 1967, I walked into my office and a big crack came in the glass ceiling at KG&E.

7. Involve, Initiate, Improve

I was placed in the marketing department but had community assignments as requested; both were under Kimball's Senior Vice President department.

It was an exciting time in the electric industry. KG&E had developed a program called, "Live Better Electrically" that was so successful it was purchased by General Electric. Their spokesperson was Ronald Reagan and he had been in Wichita several times giving the program recognition.

The peak use of electricity had switched to summer with the use of air conditioning. If electric heating were increased, the demand factor could be leveled. Marketing was important and I fit into the promotion of electricity as easily as I had selling Girl Scout cookies.

Marketing it was a good subject and most people liked the electric utility and the reliability it provided to run every gadget rapidly being put on the market and making work and life easier.

When I had the initial interview with Senior Vice President Elmer Hall, who was also on the Girl Scout Board of Directors, he handed me a full file folder that read "Atomic Energy…the Power to Power Electric Generating Stations." He told me to keep it and he would send information to keep me up-to-date for KG&E was going in that direction. I did as he told me and kept a separate file in a storeroom.

In 1968 came Eisenhower's push for "Atoms for Peace," which spurred on Admiral Hyman Rickover's nuclear navy and the construction of nuclear fueled electric generating stations.

The first major promotion assignment was to set up an outdoor children's program for the open house at the new Gordon Evans Generating Station. Bob Rives, directing the event from Corporate Communications, took me to the plant to tour and discuss what would be needed.

As I entered the station, the plant manager told me I would need a hard hat to go any farther and shoved one at me. I put it on and continued the tour with Rives. As we were leaving, the manager asked me if I was coming back and if I would be wearing a dress. I told him that was my normal work attire and, yes, I would be back. It seems he didn't allow women on the site and even had a male secretary to prove a point. I took off the hard hat, handed it to him and told him to shelve it for the next visit. He was not happy.

He wasn't the only one facing a female on board. Previously there had not been a woman supervising the work of a man. But I needed a projectionist to show the kid-cartoons. A clerk in the marketing department knew the equipment and was assigned the task. While I had not felt badly for the plant manager, this first was harder. I tried to go lightly and give him as much space to do the job; taking directions from me was not easy.

Cartoons, cookies and Kool-Aid in the tent were a big success with the kids and on that hot Kansas summer day, many adults found reprieve in the shade with a cold drink. Kimball told me later he didn't know if it would work, but then he said that's why he'd hired me.

Because of my overtime, Byrne decided it would be all right for me to take a couple of days off since I would not have any paid vacation until I had been on the job for a year and a half. We took advantage of a long weekend and went to St. Louis to watch the Cardinals play.

I organized marketing meetings, sales-allies meetings, wrote brochures for Total Electric Open Houses, and took on other duties as assigned.

The first marketing meeting I arranged at the Lassen Hotel was a success, both the awards luncheon and the reception/dinner and keynote speaker. Following the marketing meeting a bonus trip was company sponsored for the men to Shangri-La at Grand Lake, in Oklahoma and the home economists at a location of their choice. I did not fit into either staff assignment. I was not included.

Mr. Kimball, who was not leaving until later in the day, came into the office to pick up some material to take to the "guys" and saw me at my desk. He realized that I didn't fit into the "honored" categories. He invited me to go to lunch with him at the Wichita Club and made arrangements for me to have a "personal holiday" at my choosing then and in the years to come. It turned out to be a nice way to be "left out."

The next major effort was the "Lift Better Electrically Rodeo" held in the exhibition hall of the Broadview Hotel. It was the only building in the city with a floor PSI that would accommodate the fork lifts that were featured in the show.

My signature was to go on the letter of invitation to dealers to come to an organizational meeting. I wrote the letter, Jacobshagen and Byrne edited it and, when it was time to sign, Byrne had me sign it D.B. Dilsaver for he thought that if it was signed by a woman, the dealers would not come.

We had 100 percent response to the luncheon. Byrne welcomed and handled the introductions of our staff and the dealers. Mouths flew open when D.B. became known as Donna. I quickly picked up on the agenda to give them forms to fill for participation. Everyone did.

Working with the in-house print shop, we developed a series of mailings, invitations and informational brochures to market the electric fork lift vehicles. Most food warehouses were already using them and gave strong testimonials of their efficiency.

The show was a success and so too were the printed materials. They were the first of many first place winning entries in the National Federation of Press Women Communication Contest. When the recognition to me was announced in the newspaper, I received another note from Kimball: "This is why I hired you."

I continually had assignments with community organizations, including being consecutive chairman for a number of years of the United Way kick-off drive with bands, speakers and attendance by agencies supported by the fund. Each year they gave me a plaque at the awards luncheon. Each one has my name differently – Mrs. Dick (Richard) Dilsaver. Mrs. R. L. Dilsaver. Mrs. R. Dick Dilsaver – but never Donna Dilsaver.

The NOW organization was in the spotlight, quarreling about women from pay to equal career opportunities to fashion, including burning bras, but little was being done about how to address women. Some were still Miss, some Mrs., some preferred Ms. Others finally chose to use their first name as I always had. I insisted on being addressed as Donna Dilsaver.

I was to give a speech at the Missouri Valley Electrification Council meeting in Kansas City; it would be the first industry meeting I would attend. I knew no one except the co-KG&Eers in attendance. My topic was about window displays and venue's role in sales and marketing.

I was very nervous. I'd given hundreds of speeches before without a quiver. One of the fellows told me to just imagine everyone in the audience naked, wearing absolutely no clothes, and I'd do fine.

Not good advice. As I was introduced and headed to the podium, I mentally undressed everyone and there were some weird, overweight fellows seated on the front row. I began with my opening line, "Stop the feet and start the mind," concentrate on what you are showing – a new television set, new appliances, new hand tools.

Aside from one of the Home Economists (all utilities had a staff of them) I was the first woman to speak to the group. My speech was a success, but throughout the rest of the conference whenever I'd see one of the front-row fellows, they'd be walking about with no clothes. And they just thought I had a gracious, friendly smile for them.

Work and home were daily tasks midst the unrest and upheaval in the country. Elmer Lee had been injured playing football, Ron was busy with basketball, Dick was on the copy desk and we gathered at 7 each evening for dinner. Dick had headlines and stories from the next day's newspaper by that time so conversations were always lively and enlightening. I encouraged it for I felt it was educational for the boys.

One of the most difficult years was 1968. The war raged on, polarizing the nation with poor results and many casualties in Vietnam. Martin Luther King, Jr. was killed. Bobby Kennedy was shot and died in Los Angeles while running for President. Johnson announced he would not seek another term in office. Richard Nixon announced he would run for President. Aunt Edna died of cancer. Grandpa Bolton died after months in a home. We had planned to go to the Olympics in Mexico to watch Jim Ryun participate as we had watched him at East set a national mile-record-run. We could not afford it. Elmer Lee graduated from East High School, enrolled at WSU but was not enjoying being back in class, so enlisted in the Marines on his 18th birthday in November. Dick's battle with alcohol was in decline. It seemed major events were all negative with little of anything positive happening in our lives. Some color was about to be added.

During the years, to introduce new design and technically improved television sets, the company set up name brand TVs with a common antenna in the auditorium during the World Series. It was popular with downtown workers who brought in lunches to watch the game and evaluate the new TVs.

This year the event was bigger and better for we were introducing all major color TV sets on the market. Magnavox had a new set named "Works in the Drawer." The first without tubes, but solid state. They had a run on the distributor. Not only was my show a success, but because of the orders, the dealer let me have the floor model for cost. Since we were not going to the Olympics, I used the money we'd saved to buy it. One of the few perks I ever took advantage of for my family.

One activity that kept me on keel and very busy was the National Federation of Press Women Convention to be held in Wichita. My assignment on the local committee was to manage a news bureau. Don Granger and PRSA friend Paul Dannelley mentored me in "how to set it up." In years past, there was no central location for stories to be filed with out-of-state media. Reporters came to the center to phone stories, over-night photographs and write some for the newspaper to file on wire services. It was a learning process for me and it worked. We had unusual media cooperation and coverage for major events. I could do it again if assigned.

By comparison, the presidential campaign of 1968 with Richard Nixon against Democrat VP Hubert Humphrey was lackluster. Lyndon Johnson had made such a muck of things in Vietnam, his Great Society was bankrupting the country. The "silent majority" came out enough to vote to put Republicans in office.

Dick and I were invited to a political chat party at Don and Mary Granger's home. Phil and Nancy Kassebaum were also there. I'd met Nancy when she was a volunteer at the Institute of Logopedics and later when we attended the Governor's Inauguration in Topeka. Mary got tired of Phil's snapping at Nancy and told him one more time and his next drink would go down his neck. From that evening on, Nancy and I stayed in contact for one cause or another. That evening was one of the more interesting political events of the season.

Our Live Better Electrically marketing efforts were

successful throughout the service area. During the fall we all had assignments for the Marketing and Awards meeting for staff and electric business allies.

My assignment was the awards luncheon and the reception and banquet. I had coordinated many annual meetings for the Girl Scouts but this was totally different. The "allies" provided the open bar reception prior to the banquet. This was different for me.

The free drinks were flowing even greater than any Press Conference I'd attended. When we still had an hour to go, Mr. Evans, KG&E president, came to me and told me to "shut this place down," with still a half-hour to go. I found my VP Byrne, told him and he directed me to tell the bar tenders they could serve one drink only to each in line and then close. That was probably the least popular action I ever took at the company.

I was anxious for the holidays to be over and move on to new assignments. The company had me very active in professional and community activities serving on United Way, Red Cross, Press Women, and any other group where Kimball decided he needed a volunteer. There were days it seemed I had little time to do my assigned work.

As my work increased, Grace retired, and she and Dad took their camper to southern Texas for the winters. Other times they were frequent over-nighters with us when they had early doctor appointments. They had keys to the house and felt welcome and free to stay anytime.

Thelma and Vince Dilsaver were also frequent weekend visitors throughout the years. They enjoyed being with us for Thelma's annual teacher's meetings, birthdays, Easter weekend and any other time they could get away from Kensington for a few days.

In the spring of 1969, Dick was covering more business and less copy desk work. He was also very excited about having his childhood friend come to Wichita and the two of them would drive to Kensington for their high school reunion where Captain Kent Carroll was to be the featured speaker for his 25th anniversary.

The trip did not go well for Dick's drinking problem was magnified more that weekend than at any other time. He was embarrassed but Kent was gracious and continued his contact with encouragement.

Richard Nixon was now president and had escalated the Vietnam War even more than where Johnson had left off. It is an important time in American history for the unrest, hate and anti-government sentiment had everyone on edge. Even conversation at coffee break became difficult.

The most positive event was putting men on the moon in 1969. Kennedy had made the commitment; scientists and engineers had come together to design the vehicle; Congress had argued, but continued to fund the costly project; and we did it.

Space to earth changed. Neil Armstrong walked on the moon on July 17, 1969.

That month, Ron also changed. He went with Ed and his grandparents to visit Cleah's family in California. He watched the moonwalk with them and took his first airplane ride alone. He came home more mature and independent.

With both grandmothers in the care of others, Elmer in the Marines in Vietnam and Dick's reaction to it, I took some relief as the decade ended and moved on to a new calendar.

Sportscope column from Friends University Life newspaper, and the photo used for illustration.

Official press passes

Sports reporter presenting Eagle award for small town baseball at Lawrence Stadium.

BEST TOWN TEAM—Ben Stremel, left, is given the town team award by Miss Donna Bolton, member of The Eagle Sport staff, on behalf of The Eagle, donor of the cup going to the club which finished highest among small town clubs in the Kansas baseball event.—(Eagle Staff Photo.)

Editor of the Talisman yearbook, presented copy to City Mayor Walt Keeler.

CITY GETS FRIENDS YEARBOOK — A copy of the Talisman, Friends university yearbook, was presented to the city Wednesday at a Talisman chapel session in alumni auditorium. Mayor Walt Keeler was on hand to accept the book, which will be filed in the Wichita Public library. Mrs. Donna Bolton Ryan, yearbook editor, presented the book while Lloyd S. Cressman, president of Friends, right, looks on.—(Eagle Staff Photo.)

With close friends from Westside Church, on a trip to Colorado, Alice Walkob, Betty and Jean Stiles.

College Senior Photo

Joyce Riggs Church, jockey story lead to feature articles, life-long friend

As editor of the Talisman, the 1954 Friends University yearbook, I called together a formal event for students and staff classmates, including faculty advisors Isabel Crabb and Cass Riggs.

FU Graduate Named To Girl Scout Staff

Mrs. Donna Ryan, daughter of Mr. and Mrs. R. H. Bolton, Rt. 8, has been appointed as a new professional staff member of the Wichita Area Girl Scout office, Mrs. L. C. Hay, office chairman, announced Friday.

Mrs. Ryan was graduated from Friends University in 1954 with a major in sociology. While attending the university she was active in the Women's Athletic Assn., and Sports Club and was a member of Iota Theta Mu. She was sports editor of "The Life," school newspaper, editor of "The Talisman," yearbook, and editor of the student directory.

She is the widow of Ronald Ryan and has a 2-year-old son, Ronny.

DONNA RYAN

Joined Girl Scout professional staff as Public Relations Director.

First year staff, Eleanor Whitlow, Dolores Crum, me, Dagmar Magill, Mary Chesnut, Susie Babb, Betsy Long, Jayne Smith, Executive Director (Dolores and Mary continue to be monthly lunch bunch).

Magazine Coordinator, PR staff, Girl Scout Roundup in Idaho, with campers in 1965.

Round up field office.

Board meeting with members to initiate Cowtown Guide Program.

Camp director at Girl Scout Little House, yearly assignment.

123

25-Year Career at Kansas Gas & Electric.
a. Marketing, selling Total Electric, Industrial, Commercial, Residential 1967-1973.
b. & c. Assignment expanded to include education, teacher workshops, student symposiums, public programs and assigned to Nuclear Energy Women, Women in Energy 1973-1990.
d. Last day in office at time of earlier than normal retirement.

Working with Artist Blackbear Bosin during construction, installation and dedication of Wichita and Sedgwick County's symbol, "Keeper of the Plains," shown at head during assembly.

The dedication program, at right, May 18, 1974, won a First Place in National Federation of Press Women Contest.

"Keeper," at left, on the ground, now raised 40' above the ground at the confluence of the Little and Big Arkansas River.

Celebrating the 15th anniversary of the Keeper, May 1989.

Utility companies support Women in Energy.

Dr. Margaret Maxey and Women in Energy were welcomed to KG&E by sign and in person. Shown (L to R) are: LaNelle Frey, Kansas Electric Cooperatives, Dr. Maxey, Kay Johnson, KG&E environmental technician, Sharon Adams, Data Control and chairman of the meeting, Donna Dilsaver, KG&E communications specialist and regional chairman of Women in Energy, and Verna Ridgeway, KG&E assistant vice-president.

Dr. Maxey Tells Women "Future Includes Nuclear"

Wolf Creek Generating Station came on line September 5, 1985, operating successfully since. A site of pride.

Dilsaver

Dilsaver's responsibilities include public education programs. Her many hours of work outside the office for the National Science Teachers Association's convention held in Wichita last October helped earn her this honor. Dilsaver was instrumental in arranging a Student Science Day at WSU in conjunction with the convention. NSTA officials hope to make student participation a part of all their conventions.

An honor for Kansas Science Teachers Association.

1982 World's Fair, with emphasis on energy, Knoxville, Tennessee.

On tour, Germany Nuclear Generating Station, 1981.

 Women in Energy, an outgrowth of Nuclear Energy Women, presented programs to thousands of women throughout the nation calling attention to the importance of their attention to our energy-based economy.

Women recognize importance of nuclear energy at conferences. With Dr. Margaret Maxey, Dixy Lee Ray, PhD and former Washington governor, and Senator Nancy Landon Kassebaum.

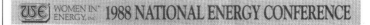

Senator Kassebaum

Dixy Lee Ray

Taking a break in Scottsdale, Arizona, before speaking to NEW and in Chicago to American Nuclear Society and Atomic Industrial Forum.

Presenting Women in Energy Achievement Award, 1980, to Margaret Bush Wilson, President of NAACP.

Honored as WE Founder.

Dilsaver honored as WE founder

Donna Dilsaver, administrator communication & educational services in Corporate Communications, is the founder of a nationwide group of professional women in the energy industry and related fields — Women in Energy.

Dilsaver founded Women in Energy in 1978. It has since grown from charter membership of 40 in four states to nearly 400 members across 26 states. At the Women in Energy National Energy Conference August 25 in Chicago, Dilsaver was honored for her commitment and effective leadership of the organization.

The award Dilsaver received is to be known as the Donna Dilsaver Award, in the founder's honor. The award was established to be presented annually to a Women in Energy member who meets the criteria of professionalism, success in networking, success in communication skills, success in Women in Energy promotion and member recruiting and all-around dedication to Women in Energy.

Donna Dilsaver

Also attending the national conference from KG&E was **Eddie York**, technician III, Operations-Training. York has been a Women in Energy member since 1986 and is the incoming president of the Kansas chapter.

Originator of the Wichita Wing Walker Award to recognize women in leadership as role models for young women. Presented by Forum for Executive Women.

Olive Ann Beech, first "Walker" recipient and Beech Aircraft Company CEO; Babs Mellor, sculptor of the award; Donna Dilsaver, creator of the award; Captain Susan Darcy, Production Test Pilot and featured speaker.

Senator Nancy Kassebaum, second recipient of the Wing Walker Award, presented by Kristen Ryan.

NANCY LANDON KASSEBAUM
KANSAS

United States Senate
WASHINGTON, D.C.

Greetings to the second annual gathering of Wichita women — gathered this year to honor a woman whose dedication and abilities have made the name Beech and quality aviation synonymous around the world.

Congratulations to all at the dinner — but a very special greeting to a woman I greatly admire — Olive Ann Beech.

With appreciation and warmest wishes,

Nancy

Letter from Senator Nancy Kassebaum Baker.

Letter from Olive Ann Beech, President/CEO of Beechcraft Company

May 3, 1990

Mrs. Donna Dilsaver
Forum for Executive Women
% K G & E
310 N. Market
Wichita KS 67202

Dear Donna:

I won't go into detail about "Wichita Women's Night" but it was very well done and I appreciated the program and the interesting remarks by the group. Of course, the speaker was outstanding and I agree, "we can do anything," which you reflected so calmly and interesting.

The highlight of the evening was the Wing Walker #1 sculpted by Babs Mellor. The enthusiasm of the sponsors was heartwarming. Thanks. I am grateful, too, for Senator Nancy's suggestion and encouragement.

Slowly We Go ----

Olive Ann Beech

OAB:clg

A loaned executive from KG&E to the Convention/Visitors Bureau, I first filled the position of Manager of News Bureau for the Miss USA Pageant in 1990 and continued through 1994.

Press Pass for use during pageant.

Pinning official pageant badge on TV personality Dick Clark.

132

Sharing desk with Clark and Leeza Gibbons during work sessions.

Nadia Comaneci, Donna and Bart Connor back stage at the pageant.

Everyone dresses formal for the Crowning Night.

Miss World and Miss Teen USA join me back stage before telecast of pageant.

PR Co-Chairman and friend Marge Setter attend Final Night.

8. Women's Voice in Energy – a Nuclear Challenge

The first year of the decade brought many changes. I attended my first Al-Anon meeting with Mary in February. A very good step for me. Dick began attending AA meetings and there was hope for the two of us to keep our family together.

In the '60s I served on the speaker's bureau to build a new Convention/Civic Center in downtown Wichita. It was being completed in time for the Wichita Centennial, one of Kimball's ideas. Organizations were gearing up for special events to fill the spring calendar with something for everyone, every day.

A local but nationally renowned Indian artist, Blackbear Bosin, was in the hospital. He was also a close friend of KG&E Senior Vice President Elmer Hall. When Hall visited him he was not in good spirits. Hall dashed out to an art supply store, bought some paper and art pencils and told him to get to work on designing a sculpture he'd talked so much about doing.

Much to Hall's delight, during the week Blackbear did just that, he came up with a drawing of what he wanted a very large Indian chief to be. But it was a flat drawing. Hall took it back to the drafting/engineering department and assigned Martin Colstrum to engineer it into a three-dimensional structure. It would take him two years to complete the task. Hall kept me posted on the progress and kept me involved with the project.

Hall also sent me a very large packet of up-to-date information on the construction of nuclear power plants across the country. He called me to his office one day and asked if I was reading the nuclear material he had been sending me for the company was going to soon start building the next generating station, a nuclear one.

The company was in the midst of building a mine-mouth coal generating station at LaCygne north of Fort Scott, Kansas. It was a costly adventure, but not too much about it was being covered. It was a new subject for me and I was still in the marketing division of the company and didn't give it much thought.

I was busy helping the Home Economists with one of the last theater cooking schools the company would hold. A good friend of mine, Kathleen Kelly, home economist editor was the featured chef. The theater was packed. We had door prizes enough for everyone to go home with something if only a large bag of groceries.

It was also to be one of the last large stage events at the grand Miller Theater. Later in the year it was razed to make way for the Fourth National Bank's parking garage. Downtown Wichita was changing fast but they were tearing down many of its finest buildings in the process.

In the fall, I chaired the United Way Sound-off for the 12th time. This year would be bigger and better for it would be held in the plaza of the still-under-construction civic auditorium. When we arrived to make arrangements, I asked where the outside electoral outlets were located. There were none.

I went back to the office and got our underground engineer to help us mark where the conduits needed to come out of the foundation. He marked them with a big red marker. Someone forgot to tell the concrete men who were pouring the plaza the next morning. Everything got covered up and to this day you must use the electric sign pole or come out of the building.

A group of young Beatle-type musicians were to play the warm-up music. By the time they got all the speakers, cords and connections in place, they had time for one song before the speakers began. We had all youth organizations in attendance to total more than 2,000 cheering Boy Scouts,

Girl Scouts, Campfire Girls, YMCA, YWCA and a host of family tagalongs to cheer the lighting of the torch. As far as I know, it was the largest kick-off ever staged for the event.

When I was president of Wichita Press Women, we needed a project to pull the group together for hosting the Kansas Press Women state meeting. The coming year was the 25th anniversary of WPW. I wanted a nationally known journalist and started making necessary contacts.

By recruiting sponsors and getting some help from our congressman, we secured Liz Carpenter, President Johnson's feisty Press Secretary. She turned out to be a real drawing card. When I introduced her, I asked, is there possibly any one in the audience who does not know this lady? No hands. When she started to speak, she turned to me and said, well, is there?

The total conference was a success and one still remembered by those in attendance.

Dick went with me to Greenfield Village, Michigan, to the National Federation of Press Women Convention. We hardly paid any attention to the sessions and Dick stayed holed up in our hotel room for the Watergate hearings were in full progress. One of the speakers asked, What is the number one question the Press has today. Silence. I finally asked, will Nixon resign his office? The session totally went out of control as we all dashed to the bar area to catch up on the latest news. I couldn't have yelled FIRE and had a faster exit.

Not only was havoc being played on the political scene with the very top offices in question, but in October 1973 came the first oil embargo by the OPEC countries dropping our oil supply by 5 percent. The disruption caused long lines at gas stations, prices jumped overnight, heating oil and natural gas prices escalated. The production of electricity with natural gas was challenged.

To KG&E's credit, providing ample supply of electricity was the new coal generating station, which had just come on line. Enough extra capacity was available to keep the region in adequate electricity. A timely addition that almost pulled the company under to finance.

In March 1973, KG&E filed the appropriate and legal papers to build the Wolf Creek Nuclear Generating Station. Life for every employ would change over the next decade, some more than others. Mine more than I ever imagined when Hall gave me the Nuclear file my first week on the job.

Energy was getting much more attention by educators who were asking how they could teach younger students about energy conservation. Using five-day colorful fliers for a week's study, we developed a program with used electric meters to teach students how electricity was metered, how to read it and know how much electricity they were using. Also, how to conserve electricity at home, work and school, and what fuels were used in the production.

Working with the USD science curriculum directors, we sponsored training to teachers and provided tours of our generating stations near Wichita for middle and high school students. We funded programs at Rea Woodman Elementary School with focus on energy programs. The company also provided funds to develop an energy display at the old city library building   the Omnisphere.

As security at night was becoming a concern across the nation, the Edison Electric Institute, along with others in the industry, produced a film narrated by actor Raymond Burr, "Light the Night." At lunch, I mentioned it to Granger as he talked about problems in the city and mentioned Captain Bobby Stout of the Wichita Police Department and his public programs.

Granger suggested I call Stout and tell him about the film. I called, we went to lunch and discussed how a program could be established in Wichita. Just adding a 40-watt porch light to alternating front and back homes could provide security for neighborhoods and police.

We began organizing to include schools with the superintendent of schools to distribute fliers asking for cooperation in one area of each quadrant of the city. We developed a marketing plan and were ready to print materials to launch a citywide program.

That week the nation was hit by the 1973 oil embargo. Energy conservation was the major thrust and no promotion of energy, especially electricity, would be encouraged. The program was scrapped.

To this day there are still Light the Night programs in neighborhoods across the city. The safety it provides is logical. Always was.

These programs were major changes for the available staff who had in the past given classes on how to use electric appliances from ranges to food freezers, to washers and dryers and an assortment of new gadgets coming on the market every year. Our community work was declining and energy conservation programs increasing.

The country's Bicentennial Committee had begun making plans and funding specific projects. An application had been made earlier by the Wichita Centennial Committee to underwrite part of the expenses for construction of the Blackbear Bosin sculpture "Keeper of the Plains."

The committee granted the request for $25,000. Boy Scouts began selling medallions for $2 each to raise the other half. Contributions from industry, individuals and City Hall were added to the pot. KG&E would donate the land at the confluence of the Little and Big Arkansas River for a prominent position on the grounds of the newly constructed Mid-American All-Indian Center on the river banks.

I began working with our longtime friend Blackbear and the Metal Orchestral firm building the 40-foot Indian made of Cor-Ten steel, a material that would rust into a natural color.

The committee making arrangements for the dedication event was late getting details in place. I went to their meeting at 3 p.m. at the Chamber of Commerce office on Thursday. The event was to take place Saturday. They had not thought of a printed program until that moment.

In shock, I volunteered to see what our in-house print shop could do. We enlisted the help of a commercial artist, I found pictures and, by the end of the day, had a design in mind. The next day I went to the library, found river information and other details to write the copy. It went to the typesetter that afternoon. By Friday afternoon it was being printed.

The dedication program became a souvenir of the event and won first prize for me in the National Federation of Press Women Communication Contest.

Highlights in 1975 included Ron's graduation from WSU with high honors. Because of his celebration, I could not attend Cleah's marriage to Art Palmer in California. And two weeks later Debra and Bill Parkhurst were married.

Nixon resigned, Gerald Ford forgave him, and the door opened for Jimmy Carter to waltz into the White House. An event that was to have a major impact on energy and my career.

The company was well under way in filing for water rights, land and thousands of federal regulations to build a nuclear power pant. Since Carter said he had served in Rickover's nuclear navy, everyone in the industry thought he was in agreement with the development of nuclear generation.

Shortly after taking office, Ralph Nader and Amory Lovins had a meeting with him in the Oval Office and our energy policies changed overnight. He took on an energy conservation stance and almost brought energy production to a halt.

Late in 1977, while riding up in the elevator, Ralph Fiebach, KG&E president, asked Bob Rives, my VP, if he had asked me about serving on the national position. Rives replied, no, but he would and asked me to step into his office. An opportunity of a lifetime was offered.

The Atomic Industrial Forum was organizing a group of women to form a national task force, Nuclear Energy Women, to address many issues being asked by women, a public needing information. Westinghouse had been re-searching opinion about the production of electricity from nuclear fueled generating stations. They learned that when women were given the same facts as men, their opinion was positive. However, much of the information they were re-ceiving was from women's magazines, hardly a technical source.

I was being asked to be the Regional Chairman for Kansas, Missouri, Oklahoma and Arkansas. Time, travel and expenses would be covered by the company were I willing to serve. Rives gave me the contact information with AIF and my task began the moment I reached my office and my telephone in November 1977.

A large packet of information arrived in January with much energy information but few names of professional women contacts in the four states.

In March, I attended my first NEW meeting followed by the AIF semi-annual meeting in Los Angeles. There I connected with one from my area, a former Wichita Eagle reporter now working with an advertising agency assigned to the account of Union Electric in Saint Louis, Missouri. That was a start.

When I returned, using the Edison Electric Institute directory, I wrote letters to CEOs with copies to public rela-tions managers of all the investor-owned utilities and state electric cooperatives in the four-state area seeking names of potential members.

I asked that their representatives be professional women, exempt from overtime, available to travel at company expense and be in a position to speak to company policy at the conference table.

I had no budget, no plan of action nor program until the group could develop them. The organization would be designed to meet the needs of those participating.

That was a first in the electric industry. I made follow-up calls to my letters within a week of the mailing. In Arkansas, where they were operating the nuclear generating plant, Arkansas One, a VP of operations told me he had a secretary that had put together a successful luncheon for women, could she serve. Can she travel and speak for company policy? No, he would check further and get back with me.

In Missouri, they were building Callaway One, a sister plant to our Wolf Creek Generating Station and about a year ahead of us in construction. Union Electric gave me my contact Barbara's name. Kansas City Power and Light was checking.

In Oklahoma, Oklahoma Power and Light was not interested in nuclear power and would not be interested in such an organization. Tulsa Power and Light was filing with the Nuclear Regulatory Commission to build Black Fox. They were interested but needed time to assess personnel and would be back with me when they did.

Kansas Power and Light in Topeka was not involved with the Wolf Creek Station so I did not pursue them.

The letters and follow-up contacts left little doubt that I would not relent until I had qualified staff to serve on the Regional Task Force of NEW.

I attended the next NEW meeting in Houston and learned that others were having the same recruiting problems I was facing. There were so few women in professional positions except for those who still had Home Economists in business and those had been almost eliminated unless they were doing energy conservation programs. Most were not giving general energy programs and not involved with the nuclear operations.

Response from a number of utilities indicated a reluctance to support a group focusing only on nuclear fuel when they used a mix of coal, natural gas, oil and nuclear. It seemed if we were to have an effective communication effort about energy, we needed to include all fuels, energy conservation and be willing to provide programs to men's groups as well as women.

The outgrowth of that thinking process came Women In Energy. There were dozens of women's organizations made up of professional women in construction, engineering, banking, journalism, business, attorneys, medical professions – all because they were not included in the major men's organizations of those professions.

The intention was not to become an auxiliary for any men's group but to stand alone, with our own design, programs and management. We needed to address all forms of energy, not focused on nuclear fuel but including it intentionally in the fuel mix to assure energy independence in the future.

144

9. Retiring Midst a Beauty Pageant

One Saturday I walked into the office at 8 in the morning and left late in the afternoon. I had written the by-laws for a new organization that could be incorporated as an educational not-for-profit 501(C)3 in each state under the umbrella of the four-state region. We would have membership dues, publications of our own design, a monthly newsletter to grow the membership and provide programs in each state. I just needed people to sign on to the concept and a steering committee to organize each state.

If I could get Kansas organized first, it could be used as a guide for the others. KG&E was in agreement for we needed to separate the effort from liability to the utilities. Our own incorporation would address that problem. Help came from Jim Haines, an attorney who was working rates for the nuclear project, but took time to help with the forms needed to proceed.

Mr. Wall, president of Kansas Power and Light, had not been contacted about NEW, but we needed them on board since they covered so much of the state with electricity and natural gas. I called his office, asked when he might be available for five minutes to talk to me about a professional women's organization in the utility business. With so much attention being given to women in the workplace, she scheduled the meeting.

He would be in the office the next day. I had the two-hour morning drive to mentally write a five-minute presentation to one of the most popular businessmen in the state. I arrived a few minutes early to freshen up, breathe deeply and walk in to be greeted by his secretary. She began asking questions about the nature of my call. Fortunately, Mr. Wall stepped out of his office, offered me a fresh cup of most welcome coffee and asked, "What may I do for you?"

I told him about the concept of Women in Energy, covered briefly the Carter administration energy policy which was likely to worsen, and that I needed the names of women on his professional staff who could be available to initiate a statewide effort of energy education to adults. I did that in my allotted five minutes.

He smiled at me across the desk and said, "You are serious and it makes sense. I think you can pull it off. What do you need from me?" After another 20 minutes of covering my memorized list, he followed me to the elevator and said, "Hell ova deal."

Within the next year most of my work was focused on putting together a viable organization in each state, recruiting qualified members for our board of directors and presenting programs to civic, service and professional organizations.

I could write an entire book about initiating, directing and growing Women in Energy. I'll touch only on a few highlights of the next four years.

One of the most meaningful NEW meetings was held in Washington State. We toured the Atomic Energy Reservation, yes, the place where I'd been lost at the time of the Girl Scout Round-up. We were welcomed to Exxon's Laboratories, saw spent fuel being reprocessed, toured the area of nuclear waste facilities and given firsthand information from scientists working for the government, military and industry. What an enlightenment.

With less than 20 in attendance, we had an informed and enthusiastic reception and conversation with Dr. Dixy Lee Ray. Her position as governor of Washington had given her and the state a major role in the nuclear industry. The meaningful session was the beginning of a long association with her.

In January 1979, the NEW and AIF meetings were being held in Washington, D.C. It was the first week the new

Kansas senator and longtime friend Nancy Landon Kassebaum was sworn into office. Between meetings, she had her staff assistant tour me through the capitol building.

One of the more interesting stops was at VP Walter Mondale's office, stacked with file boxes and the bathroom door standing open. I told my guide it was interesting to see the VP of the United States had a throne so nearby. He laughed, closed the door, and said it is a small space.

Nancy took me to lunch in the Senate dining room. That was special, but so too were all the well known list of senators stopping by our table to welcome Nancy into the Senate. She was the first female elected in her own right to the Senate.

The next day I had an early morning tour of the White House. We were held in the Gold Room as we watched President and Mrs. Carter being escorted to the helicopter to attend the funeral services in New York City for former Vice President John D. Rockefeller. An interesting place to be on an historic day in the capitol.

In the afternoon I kept my scheduled meeting with Rep. Dan Glickman, a courtesy call normally made when anyone from our company was in Washington. I anticipated a greeting and go. I spent more than a half-hour in his office talking about energy in Kansas, including his interest in ethanol and how it could be made economically a serious addition to the fuel mix.

He was due shortly for a House vote, asked me to walk with him, which I did. As we exited his office, the hall was packed with farmers who had driven tractors en masse to Washington to protest farm prices. I was flattered until I realized I was a shield for Glickman to get to the chambers for his vote. We parted at the end of the tunnel.

It was well timed, for in the tunnel boarding a train was Senator Robert Dole. As I said hello, he said, yes, you've been trying to contact me to see if Elizabeth could speak to your group next fall in Kansas City. He assured me he would have staff contact me to work out the details.

That night I heard sirens, looked out the hotel window and saw the president's car and procession en route back to the White House after having had dinner at the Chinese Embassy with the visiting Vice Premier Deng Xiaoping and his wife.

I didn't have much time for touring the city and the Air Museum at the Smithsonian was upper most on my list. I took the subway from the hotel to the Plaza. As I approached the building, the Chinese delegation with Deng Xiaoping was leaving. He and delegation stopped, turned and looked at me. Not a one of them was more than 5 foot tall. I was wearing 3-inch heel boots, a three-piece camel-hair ensemble with full length cape, a 5-foot-10inch slender image coming solo their direction. I surely must have seemed the image of a moving Statue of Liberty to them.

As I entered the building, the first exhibit on a waist-high pylon was a piece of a rock from the moon. The guard said the Chinese chairman was the last to touch it, now you have the honor. Then said, now you and the Chinese chairman have joined forces on the moon.

It was a great time to be in Washington for everyone was in town. A major endorsement with staff assistance from Union Electric in St. Louis, Missouri at the meeting gave Women in Energy much needed assistance.

The four-state area under the umbrella of Women in Energy was providing a major communication effort to inform the public about the need to develop all forms of fuel to feed the country's energy based economy. Nuclear energy was always included in the fuel mix to accomplish the goals of Nuclear Energy Women.

Then came the unexpected by the nuclear industry. First, in March, came the release of the Jane Fonda/Jack Lemon movie, "China Syndrome." A hoax about a possible meltdown at a nuclear power plant that would burn all the way to China. It was decided that some of us including those on the Wolf Creek staff would attend a matinee at a downtown theater.

There weren't many people in the theater, mostly us. The fellows from the nuclear navy working for us laughed most of the way through it as mistakes after mistakes of technical information were portrayed. It would be devastating to the nuclear energy industry if Fonda had the same result as she'd had in Vietnam. Two nuclear experts, she and Lemon, if the gullible public seemed to want to believe them.

As we walked back to the office, I commented to Dr. Robert Hagan (Dr. Bob), a product of Rickover's nuclear navy and a major expert in the field, we had better come up with some one-liner sound bites for the media if we're going to survive this masterful attack. He chuckled and said, show them to me when you get them written.

I didn't have time to give them much thought for I was busy at Wichita State University getting ready for the Kansas Academy of Science meeting which I had helped program and had the company sponsor. Working through the American Nuclear Society, I had been able to secure Dr. Ralph Lapp as featured speaker for the opening session. Dr. Lapp was nationally recognized authority on nuclear issues for he had been a member of the Manhattan Project. I was to pick him up at the hotel at 9:30 a.m.

Then the second shoe dropped on the industry. On March 29, 1979, I arrived at the office at 7:30, everyone was gathering in the auditorium for a briefing. There had been an incident at Three Mile Island nuclear generating facility in Harrisburg, Pennsylvania. Charts and pictures were blown-up on the screen with nuclear engineers showing and telling as much as they knew about what had happened. They kept assuring us that the radiation safety shield covering the plant had not been breached and there was no evidence that any radiation was outside the containment area.

With that information, I left to pick up Lapp and had an overwhelming education in the 30-minute drive to WSU about what had happened and how the incident could be controlled. However, he said, the radiation hysteria with the news media was unreal and would have to be addressed soon by scientists who were qualified to speak about the incident. He was most upset but was anxious to give his speech and talk to knowledgeable scientists about the event.

When we arrived at WSU, I took him to the hall where he was to be introduced by the KAS president and to speak within the half-hour.

The WSU Information Officer met me and took me to a nearby office. He said, Dr. Lapp had an urgent call. I told him I'd respond and get a message to Dr. Lapp. The call was from CBS; Walter Cronkite's staff was calling to get Dr. Lapp back to Washington for the six o'clock evening news. Lapp was being introduced to the audience.

Since I had Lapp's itinerary, I was able to call the airline, changed his flight to the first one out of Wichita to Washington. The time schedule permitted a few questions from the scientists in attendance. I announced to the group why he needed to leave and to listen to CBS News that night to hear an update.

Lapp's luggage was still in my car so we headed to the airport. That night he tried to calm the commentator and the pseudo-scientist telling the public there had been no breach of the containment building and there was little danger of any radiation contamination. The "radiation hysteria" being lauded by the media was doing more damage than the accident. Although the industry has tried on a number of occasions for documentaries, CBS to my knowledge has yet to release the Cronkite interviews from that night with Lapp.

Lapp refers to the Kansas Scientists Academy meeting and TV appearance in his book, "The Radiation Controversy."

The nuclear industry changed overnight and a lower-than-elementary science mentality cloaked the public causing generating stations almost completed and those on the planning boards halted. Although President Carter had said he was a Rickover-Navy trained nuclear engineer, he failed to be straightforward with the American people and let the activists rather than the scientists and engineers direct the nuclear future. Thankfully he left the nuclear navy alone, a topic we had been firmly instructed to not mention in any of our industry presentations. We needed our nuclear navy left untouched by civilian unreality.

Requests for energy programs increased and some women were promoted into a professional status so they could participate. We were at the right place at the right time.

It was a most eventful year for me on the job, but mainly on a personal note. Ron and Kathy were living in Dallas, Texas, and there on May 15, 1979, my first grandchild was born, Katherine Shawn Ryan. I took a week of vacation at the end of May, took Dad and Grace with us to see Katie. They would bring her to Wichita for several visits so we could watch her grow and share in her life during the next four years they lived in Dallas.

The high interest rates causing economic chaos in the country hit all construction with a massive slow-down and none was hit harder than the electric utilities. Most were at the point-of-no-return with nuclear facilities. The Energy Act of 1978, designed by the Carter Administration, directed utilities to abandon the use of natural gas for electric generation. It forced switching to coal and nuclear. Wind, solar, and biofuels were further into the future if ever economically possible.

An important meeting for the industry was in Boston at the Copley Hotel in Boston. After the NEW meetings, there was an evening break before the AIF sessions would begin in the morning.

George Bush was in the midst of his campaign for president and would have a rally at the hotel that night. A group of college students were gathering outside the Copley with anti-nuclear energy signs for a demonstration against Bush's endorsement of using nuclear fuel in the nation's energy mix.

In visiting with the demonstrators, an AIF staff member learned that they were being paid $10 an hour with a four-hour minimum by Ralph Nader's anti-nuclear organization. Some of the NEW members decided to make pro-nuclear placards of their own to mix with the group for media coverage.

Street marching was not my style. I slipped away and went into the hotel mezzanine so I could watch the rally from a vantage point. A few chairs were near the railing where a woman was sitting alone. I sat beside her, introduced myself. She told me her daughter was one of the young people helping with the rally and she'd come to see her.

She began asking questions. I told her what was going on outside the hotel and had decided I'd rather be inside to see Mr. Bush.

A lady came in from a side door to be seated next to my new friend. I heard the doors lock and smiled with satisfaction that I was well situated. The two women visited about children, walking their dogs and general conversation of common interests. Then the friendly lady asked me to tell her, pointing to the lady next to her, about the group demonstrating outside the hotel. I did.

The lady slapped her thigh and said, I can't wait to tell George.

Oh, my. I had not seen her in person before but quickly realized the lady I'd been chatting so casually with was none other than Barbara Bush. She gave me a Bush for President button, which I still have. The rally began. We parted with an exchange of good wishes, she suggesting they could use active supporters in Kansas. Her autographed book, which I received later, is in my study.

Our organizations, both NEW and WE, were growing well and our programs were receiving positive receptions as we covered energy information and the need to continue to develop supplies for the future.

The fall meeting was held in Scottsdale, Arizona. A meaningful meeting with a new slide presentation developed for mass use. Cleah came over from California to spend a couple of days with me for I was to go directly to Chicago for the AIF and American Nuclear Society (ANS) joint meeting. I would be making the presentation for our organization, giving an update and enlisting support from both groups.

It is true, women have more problems knowing what to wear than men. I had long since learned that the higher the officer the darker the suit. CEOs wear black, dark navy or dark pin-stripe, next management level wears lighter navy, lighter pin-stripe, gray or very dark brown, next level at a meeting and many academics wear browns, sports jackets, much more casual.

I needed to make a statement and wrap all of the above into one image. Because I was gone for a week of meetings, I had most colors with me. As I looked at the suits in the hotel closet, I spotted the perfect one. A bright red, well fitted suit with white silk shirt and gold jewelry would make an entrance and a statement. They could not categorize me on sight.

Did it ever. There was no dais, only a podium from which all speakers were introduced and spoke to the large hall of CEOs, managers, nuclear engineers, scientists and assorted other industry management. I was seated a couple of rows back at the side of the room. I was introduced and moved as gracefully as possible across to the podium in front of the audience. There was an intake of air as they saw me. I started speaking the moment I was in front of the microphone.

I delivered one of the most important speeches of my career and received a standing ovation from the impressive gathering of top nuclear industry management. Lynn Draper, then president of the American Nuclear Society and CEO of a Texas utility, invited me to have lunch at his table. On the way there he commented that I looked smashing in the red suit and selecting it was a stroke of genius with this group. He laughed and said, they don't know how to classify you.

The contact with Draper turned out to be valuable for he came to Wichita to a Science Teacher Conference at my request and made a lasting impression about nuclear energy to high school and college science teachers.

He and another nuclear engineer friend, Sandra Kiefer, were the two selected by the industry to follow Jane Fonda, and her then-husband, Tom Hayden, across the country making TV appearances in protest of nuclear power. The two became known as the "Truth Squad." Fonda was once heard asking a TV producer if the two entering the studio were the "Truth Squad." There was no comparison in the two of the facts but the public seemed infatuated with the famous two, knowing full well they knew nothing about nuclear generated electricity.

Women in Energy sponsored many energy conferences in Oklahoma, Missouri, Arkansas and Kansas, inviting professional women's groups, women in government, industry and academic positions. If it were an annual meeting, the Women in Energy Achievement Award was presented in addition to a prominent speaker.

In Kansas City, Mary Hudson of Hudson Oil was the awardee and U.S. cabinet member Elizabeth Dole was the speaker. Both drew positive news coverage for the local area.

In St. Louis, Margaret Bush Wilson, president of the NAACP who had led the group to endorse a strong energy policy, was the awardee and the speaker was Bioethics Professor Dr. Margaret Maxey. She also served on more industry boards of directors than any other woman in the country.

In Wichita, Governor Dr. Dixy Lee Ray was the awardee and Senator Nancy Landon Kassebaum was the speaker.

As chairman of the board of directors, I was privileged to make the awards and introduce the featured speakers.

One of my favorite meetings was held in Little Rock, Arkansas, sponsored by Arkansas Power and Light. The governor's wife was to welcome the group to the city, but Hillary Clinton had a conflict in her schedule so the mayor filled in for her. The first "no show" in our experience.

There were four of us to be on the panel for the morning session in Little Rock in the large auditorium at APL. One was a nuclear engineer professor, another a laboratory scientist, my friend Sandra Kiefer and myself.

We each made brief remarks, then the program opened for questions. Two women with four children sat on the front row and began shouting questions at the professor. He stuttered to find answers, taken back by their yelling. They didn't understand a word the scientist was saying so Sandra jumped in to try to calm them and give elementary answers. She also took other questions from attendees but the shouting prevailed.

I happened to catch a glance of myself in one of the live TV cameras in the room; my look was about the same as with Mother's old red hen. The camera caught my glance as if to say, don't think of attacking me. They attacked and I began a quiet meticulous shredding of their behavior, their mode of transportation, the abuse of their children in an adult meeting and asked to meet them outside after the session. It seemed to work and the session concluded with Sandra making her impressive, positive, reassuring closing.

During the lunch break, Charles Kelly, APL's public relations director, asked me if I would please take an hour call-in talk show on one of the radio stations before lunch. Radio, I'd do. It was a delight to share some of the questions asked and answered at the conference as well as those from callers. In the '80s there were still a few areas of Arkansas that did not have electricity. I had fun with it for I was not in my service area and I could say things no one from APL could.

As we flew from Little Rock to our next appearance at the University of Arkansas campus at Fayetteville, we regrouped to address the college students and faculty in a different tone, letting the professor and scientist answer most of the questions.

When we finished, the company plane took Sandra over to Memphis for her next appearance and I flew with the crew back to Little Rock. Back in my hotel room was a lovely bouquet of flowers with a card saying, "You Were Great!"

Kelly must have written letters before I left town for when I arrived back in the office, I had a most complimentary letter which was a copy of the one sent to Ralph Fiebach, KG&E president. I also had a note from Fiebach attached to a copy of Kelly's letter saying he was approving a merit increase in pay. It took almost an act of God to get a merit pay increase.

Kelly's handwritten P.S. on my copy simply said, "You Were Great!" Same as the flowers.

In Kansas, Women in Energy sponsored several symposiums for women, one at the Community College in Garden City, one in Wichita and one at the Parsons Community Center. B.J. Thorpe, the corporate communications administrator from Standard of Ohio and staff from Kansas State

University, joined me for the programs.

At the time Standard of Ohio was building the pipeline across Alaska. In Garden City one teacher's concern was more about the caribou than an oil supply for her car. When she asked about the interruption of the mating season, a man at the back of the room yelled, "Lady that will not be a problem!" He was right, now they have an abundance of animals taking heat treatments under the pipeline and expanding by exponential growth.

With all the opposition, it is amazing the major oil supply line was completed.

The country was still suffering from Johnson's failed Great Society, Richard Nixon's failed presidency, Ford's efforts to heal so many wounds, and the Carter Administration's blows to the nation's internal and external economic chaos and hostages in Iran, and was anxious to have a major change in Washington. Ronald Reagan, the actor who had helped us introduce the Live Better Electrically program in Wichita and had became the governor of California, was leading in the Republican race for President.

I had long since changed from my Democrat birth to Republican. I fit the observation by Winston Churchill: If you are not a liberal when you are young, you are heartless. If you are not a conservative when you are older, you are brainless. Dick told me I was just catching up with myself, that I had been more conservative than he from the day we were married.

Dick and I took our first international trip to see our granddaughter, Laura Parkhurst, who was born in Germany on February 11, 1981. We were in London shortly after Prince Charles and Princess Diana were married, and toured Scotland, Germany, Switzerland, France, Austria before coming home.

It was time for me to step down as CEO of Women in Energy to give others the opportunity to lead. NEW was holding fewer meetings as the nuclear industry began pulling back on the construction of new generating facilities.

An impressive plaque with my picture and one of the most complimentary messages of my career was presented to me in Wichita. The standing ovation from that group meant more to me than all those from others combined. A genuine tribute from my peer group.

Highlight of the year was our granddaughter, Kristen Maureen Ryan, born July 22, 1983. And Ron and Kathy moved back to Wichita for him to take a teaching position in the Graduate School of Business at Friends University. The move back was marred by a head-on collision by a drunk driver, severing Kathy's right foot. Several surgeries since have kept it attached but it is daily painful. That same week, Kathy received her master's degree from Texas Women's University, as a nurse practitioner, a job she has continuously held throughout the years.

In 1984 the National Federation of Press Women's national conference being held in Vail, Colorado, selected Energy, Economics, and Environment for their theme. I was invited to give a major afternoon session on energy.

Prior to my session, the luncheon speaker was Vail resident and former First Lady Betty Ford. She was a delightful and enlightening speaker. Among her many comments, she reminded us she was the only woman to serve as First Lady that had not campaigned with her husband for the office of President. From the time Nixon resigned until she walked in to live in the White House there was precious little preparation time. I've often wondered if that might not have been to her advantage for she seemed to enjoy the position with no preconceived notions of her job description. She could just be herself.

During the break following the luncheon, she was signing books at a table near my meeting room. I helped her unpack and stack books on the table and, as we did so, we began a relaxed chat. I told her of my experience in Al-Anon and hoped she had emphasized the positive impact on families the program can have. After a few questions, she said, no, not as much as I should, and made a note to herself to call the Betty Ford Center. I don't know if she followed up, if she did it would be another highlight to her credit. Her autographed book is in my study.

One of the last NEW and AIF meetings was held in Dallas where I spoke to the combined group. Then I voiced my disappointment that since TMI we were canceling too many of our plans for new generating stations that would be needed in another 20 years to keep up with energy demands, especially electric vehicles became more in demand to meet environmental standards as they had in London. I called attention to the devastating impact we would have in later years if we did not build at least four new oil refineries in each quadrant of the country. Our friend Dick Hoover in the oil business had provided me with reams of statistics.

And we would meet with great opposition from environmentalists if we continued the mandate from the 1978 Energy Act if we stayed on the course to exchange natural gas generation for coal fueled plants. No one was going to like the belch if the emissions could not be controlled.

A Texas oil man came up to me following the meeting and asked, when do you see your doomed report becoming a reality? I guessed, in my lifetime, about 25 years from now – that would be about 2009. How I wished that had become a reality.

The work on a national level brought recognition and I was included in the publications "Who's Who in the Midwest," "American Who's Who of Women" and the "World Who's Who of Women."

I began attending the Edison Electric Institute education conferences, the first in San Antonio, Texas. My work was shifting to focus more on the science education program being supported by utilities across the nation. Because we had been involved with all grades and curriculum in schools, it was a natural for KG&E.

Two weeks following the meeting, the family was attending the 4th of July celebration at Cessna Stadium at WSU. There were more than 100,000 in attendance. It had been a great night until the wind came up as the fireworks illuminated the sky. Unfortunately, we were seated at the top end of the stadium when wind swept fireworks into the crowd. I had just moved my granddaughter Laura from my lap to Phyllis so she could move out into the aisle. As she took her, a cylinder exploded on my foot. The concussion knocked me out and I was carried on a stretcher from the 60th row up to an ambulance and taken to Wesley Medical Center.

A medical attendant poured water on my wounded foot. It was excruciatingly painful. When I came to, my brother Raymond, who was also checking on Steve, his son, came to the gurney, took my hand and said, "Breathe deeply, Sis, and it won't hurt so badly."

I was off work with an infection and then skin-graft surgery until after Labor Day, then on crutches for the rest of the month. I edited the new edition of the Education Catalog in the hospital and at home so it was printed before I could return to work. I was off the crutches in time for Dick's mother's family reunion in Kensington the last weekend in September.

As we drove home, I told Dick since it was getting late it would not be necessary to go to Geneso to see Raymond and family. He said he thought we should. We did. They had been doing fall chores to clean the garden and prepare the storm windows for fall and winter weather. As we were leaving, Raymond gave me some small pumpkins from his garden for me to make Jack-o'-lanterns with my grandchildren.

As we went to the car, he gave me his casual hug, but this time a harder one and said, "Sis, I love you very much. Thanks for all you do for my family and for coming to see us." I almost cried. It was different for him.

Those were his last words to me. The next morning, I had returned from coffee break, heard the manager's phone ring, went to my desk and my phone rang. Dick said, "Donna, there is no easy way to tell you this, but I must. Raymond has been killed in an accident at the salt plant where he worked in Lyons. You and Kenneth are needed there and are to meet Phyllis and the kids at the Lyons Hospital. You need to reach Kenneth at school. I'll meet you at home with things we need to take, pick up Kenneth and leave as soon as possible." It was a long five-mile drive home. We grabbed some essentials for an overnight stay and met Kenneth at school for the 90-mile drive.

Dad and Grace had arrived in Washington, D.C., to visit her son. In the next hours, I changed their airline tickets to get the next morning flight home. The most difficult thing I've ever been called upon to do was to tell Dad about Raymond's death. Our baby brother, the ill one, the one we were all charged to take care of since birth.

Kenneth and Dick saw Raymond. I did not and in the years since, I know it to have been the right decision. Dick stayed on to help Phyllis and the family. I came home to finalize arrangements at the cemetery and to talk to the news media. As I rode back with Phyllis' sister, all I could hear was Raymond saying to me, "Breathe deeply, Sis, and it won't hurt so badly." At that moment I knew why he had been with me the night of the fireworks accident and at my side in the hospital. I needed those words from him at that moment.

That week was one of the longest, most painful in my life. What had I not done to protect him? How could God take him when he had children to raise, so much to live for?

It became another time in my life to accept the mystery of what I could not control.

My major work assignments with schools had been completed and I think I somehow managed to float through the rest of the year. The memory of Raymond is still painful, a tragic accident. When it gets too much, I think of all the good years we had with him after Dad revived him from the hide-and-seek game when we were kids. He will always be a loss, a void in my life.

We had such great friends at work, at church and with the AA group. They gave us the love and support we needed at the time. Dad and Grace began coming in to spend more time with us, which helped us both.

A number of transitions that came in 1985 changed the direction of our careers. An ethical question confronted Dick with management of the newspaper and he took early retirement.

On September 5, 1985, the Wolf Creek Generating Station reached full ascension to power and began producing electricity. Construction was complete and now we switched to the operating mode. Most of our public programs that were essential were not now. School programs were needed for teachers and students, but speeches were not. My job assignment changed to Supervisor, Corporate Communication, then to Administrator, Corporate Communication.

Also that year I worked with Walt Purdy at the Edison Electric Institute in Washington, D.C., to develop RAYS, a radiation activities for youth series published by Pennsylvania State University. If we were to educate and prepare the next generation to understand nuclear fuel used in the production of electricity, we needed to strengthen their science programs.

Cleah's husband, Art Palmer, died in August. Kenneth, Phyllis and I took Dad and Grace to his services, which Kenneth conducted. I stayed over a week to give Dad some time with her.

Dick did some freelance writing for business publications, National Realtor, Time, Newsweek and others. He also joined the KWCH TV staff for business news reports a couple of times a week. In October, Larry Jones recruited him to be his press secretary as he made his bid in the next year for governor of Kansas.

The year was a roller-coaster ride. Our grandson, Daniel Michael Ryan, was born July 3, 1986.

Larry Jones lost his bid for governor in the primary, changing Dick's career once again.

In the fall, Dick began a new position as Corporate Communication Consultant with the Coleman Company, then to the staff, and eventually back to consultant during the next 11 years.

I was offered the position of Public Information Officer at the Wolf Creek Nuclear Generating Station. It would mean I'd move to the Burlington, Kansas area. Dick's work took him to Topeka during the winter months when the State Legislature was in session, January through April. We had a very serious discussion of how we could manage, what would we do with our home. My folks were in stable but declining health as was Thelma's living alone in Kensington.

It was a position I had very much wanted five years before, but now it seemed impossible with responsibilities and the separation it would cause in Dick and my life. We had shared a close relationship during the past decade when our children were grown. We had enjoyed closeness of grandchildren and being empty nesters was a lifestyle that suited both of us.

The decision was made. I would say no to the opportunity and stay in Wichita. Staff positions were changing to accommodate the new smaller utility business. I became editor of the company publication "Servicegraph" and increased the school programs with a library of videotapes and printed materials to assist teachers with classroom energy education programs.

They foolishly scheduled a St. Patrick's Day Parade in downtown Wichita during the week of March 17, 1987, on the assumption that everyone had moved out of the downtown Wichita district and it would not bother anyone. They learned how much business the north-south traffic pattern carried.

I was on my way back to the office from the printer. A young man with more power than patience changed lanes and smacked into my new car and gave me a seat-belt injury to my left shoulder, stretching all the ligaments out of place. Since it was an on-the-job injury, I followed strict medical procedures for three months. We tried everything to relieve the pain.

After cortisone shots failed and I did not want to take any more, Dr. Lucas decided the best thing to do was start building up the muscles to keep my shoulder blade from dropping into my rib cage. He asked me if I swam, I'd not been in a pool for 10 years. He said, you're going back until you build up to a mile a day for as long as it takes to maintain muscle strength.

In the past 21 years I have averaged swimming more than 100 miles a year and continue today. My total is more than 2,500 miles.

Community service assignments, publications and editing the monthly publication kept me busy at work. Playing with grandchildren kept me young, and Dick's increased social schedule kept me active.

In the fall, Dick kept his 25-year promise to his sister, Jo, to visit them in Australia. In the weeks before we were to leave, Dad fell and broke his hip. Our dear friend and Dick's sponsor in AA, K. Kincaid died suddenly, the third friend to pass in less than two months. We could not afford to cancel our plans and left the weekend before Thanksgiving for a four-week vacation. I was able to be gone for I had saved every day of my year's vacation time to make it possible. Dick's schedule was much more flexible.

We had a week in Sydney, Brisbane and Cannes and the Great Barrier Reef before going to Melbourne to be with Jo, Tom, Peter and Jenny. We arrived in time to go to Jenny's high school graduation. Peter was in college and working at a supermarket.

We toured the area with Jo, including going to watch the miniature penguins at Phyllis Island. Dick and I left for 10 days in New Zealand, one of our best trips together. We toured North Island and Auckland first, then to South Island and Melford Sound. Dick commented that if you did not have a spiritual experience as we floated around the sound, it wasn't likely that you ever would.

We took a three-day break before coming home on Tahiti. We met the Moores from England and had a jolly time touring and dining with them.

When we arrived home, I still had time for Christmas. Cleah, Donnie and his friend came from New Mexico and California to join us for a special holiday.

It took almost the month of January to return phone calls, schedule meetings, and catch up at work. Dick was in Topeka for the legislative committee work for four months. He usually left on Sunday night and came home Wednesday, spending Thursday in the office.

My work with the Science Curriculum directors, plant tours and the Electrical Safety programs gave us energy education at all grade levels. Meetings in Division towns of El Dorado, Newton, Arkansas City, Ft. Scott, Pittsburgh and Independence had me traveling the service area more than in previous years.

Women in Energy was still a viable organization with public programs; however, the Atomic Industrial Forum was not as active. Most of my work was directed through the

Edison Electric Institute and my work increased with Walt Purdy, education director. I began attending national education meetings sponsored by EEI and worked to develop a number of student seminars.

A Science Symposium program sponsored by KG&E with industry sponsored speakers was used as an example for other utilities. Speakers included an astronaut from Houston; a professor from Montana University covering expediential growth and its impact on energy supply; and Dr. Hubert Aliyea from Princeton University.

A newspaper reporter was shocked when the 1,000 students from across Kansas gave Dr. Aliyea a standing ovation, cheering as those watching a championship athletic contest. I explained to him these were all science students who understood every experiment this nationally known scientist had shown them. His review in the paper the next day reflected his surprise. I have since encountered some of these students and doctors, engineers, laboratory scientists in our community. Seeing them at work is rewarding for all the work and long hours it took to direct the project.

It followed soon after that the WSU staff that I had worked with were interested in having a Science Olympiad for high school science students across the state. Would KG&E sponsor it? We organized the invitations much the same as I had for Science Symposium. Engineers and other technical staff volunteered their time to judge the Saturday event. We could not get permission from the State Board of Education to participate in the national competition.

That has now changed. The Olympiad continues today and students are now permitted to compete at a national level. Kenneth's grandson, Kent, was one of the national competitors when he was in high school. He is now employed by a computer company and is in a "gee whiz" product development position.

Through the work with EEI, RAYS, an education

workbook for teachers, was produced and distributed nationally through their work with electric utilities across the country.

My next major project was updating a two-decade old educational program, The Amazing People of Kansas and The Amazing Women of Kansas. As I re-read the text it was surprising how much had changed in how we express ourselves during that short time. Most descriptions were inappropriate and certainly the two titles needed to be combined into one – The Amazing People of Kansas.

It was time consuming, but letters were sent to historical societies and librarians in all 105 counties in Kansas. As recommendations came in with pictures and a brief nomination, the production process began.

It would take most of the year to get the "People" program printed and ready for distribution to school librarians for the fall semester. By placing the books in the libraries, several disciplines had access to them.

The Kansas People Test and the booklets were also a natural for programs for civic, service and senior citizens groups. I needed to come up with a way to make it an interesting speaker's program,

While waiting after church for Dick and our friends Dorothy and Omer Belden to join me for lunch at the Amarillo Grill, I took a large paper napkin and divided it into three parts. The history, the present and the future. I had seen a program shortly before by the actress Cloris Leachman portraying women. If I could create three characters to cover the century of state history and its people, it might work.

I thought of my family's history since coming to Kansas from Roanoke, Virginia in 1872; it covered most of that time. My great-grandmother was Eliza Lucinda Kessler Craig and one of the few women to own land in her own name. Northwest High School was built on her farm. My life covered much of the development since her time and my

10-year-old granddaughter, Katie, carried promise for the future.

I combined the three for a program titled, "Lou, Me and Katie." Letters offering the program at no charge were sent to appropriate groups. Requests began pouring in and my time was quickly scheduled again back at the podium. I was averaging seven programs a week, some morning, noon and night.

As a member of the Executive Forum for Women I knew we needed exposure and wanted to sponsor a program to have Senator Nancy Kassebaum as featured speaker. I checked with Georgia Ptacek, her administrative assistant in her office across the street from mine. She laughed and said, look at that stack, all letters from groups in Wichita requesting the same thing. I asked her, "If I could put together a large dinner meeting to include all of those interested, would the Senator come?"

She said, probably if you could get them all together. I began by contacting for a location, cost, budget, and list of professional women's groups in the city. I made the proposal to the executive board and they endorsed the program. I recruited a few friends and put together one of the most impressive gatherings of professional women in Wichita in the large ballroom at the Marriott Hotel. It was a sellout. Senator Kassebaum was the speaker.

It was so successful, the executive group wanted it to be an annual event. In the spring we were thinking about what would bring women together. The Wichita River Festival had a running argument about whether a woman could serve as their ring-master, the Admiral Windwagon Smith. That was the honor position of the River Festival each May in downtown Wichita.

The male role of Admiral, most thought, should remain a man. When Marge Setter and I were going to Topeka for a Press Women meeting, I asked her what she thought of a role for a woman at the River Festival that would be all her own. Marge said she'd always wanted to do something with Amelia Earhart. We talked about that idea, but I was reluctant to have a real person in such a role.

The next week we were with frequent dinner friends, Charlie and Betty Pearson. Charlie was the originator of the Admiral Windwagon Smith at the beginning of the River Festival during the Wichita Centennial. I told them what I had been thinking about for a women's role but liked the idea of having a Wing Walker. Many women in early Wichita aviation had bravely walked on wings of airplanes at barnstorming and fair air shows. Charlie responded very positively with, it's a splendid idea but you'll have trouble with those Festival people letting a woman in the limelight.

I called a well known sculptor, Babs Mellor, and asked her if she would work with me to mold the concept into a statue for an award to an outstanding Wichita woman who could be held up as a role model for young women. She was very enthusiastic about the idea and contacted aerospace engineers to get advice on an airplane wing design with a woman standing on it.

We worked on the design at the Center for the Arts. She took the mold to her bronze artists to produce the statue. At the next executive meeting, I presented the idea to them, they grasped the opportunity, and we scheduled the next women's gathering.

It was logical that one of the nation's foremost women in aviation, Olive Ann Beech, president of Beech Aircraft Company, be presented the first Wichita Wing Walker Award. It was the second outstanding program for the executive group.

The following year, the award was presented to Senator Kassebaum. Many women in Wichita have the statue to speak to their leadership and role models for young women.

During the same month was the 15th anniversary of

the installation of Blackbear Bosin's "Keeper of the Plains." Nothing had been done for the 10th anniversary and many of the originators of the impressive Indian at the confluence of the Little and Big Arkansas River were no longer with us.

Bob Rives, Corporate Communications VP, agreed that something should be done and for me to do something about it. Although the statue was being used as an official symbol for both the city and the county, there was not an official photograph to be used by people wanting permission to use the image. The Keeper has a copyright by the Bosin family.

I contacted the promotion manager for the Wichita Eagle to co-sponsor a photo contest to produce such a picture. In May, during the River Festival, a ceremony recognizing those who were instrumental in making the statue possible were honored. A videotape was made and is now with the Art and Facilities Director at the City of Wichita.

The two events prompted the editor of the Wichita Woman newsstand paper to feature me as the cover story. It was an honor but a little embarrassing to be featured along with grocery store tabloids in every store in the city. It was a good article and gave me recognition in the community I had enjoyed in previous years.

I had been serving on the Friends University KSOF Radio Station and had been on the air with Paul Threlfall several times. He was a former Beacon photographer when I was on The Eagle sports staff. He had been news director for KAKE TV since it began telecasting. He had called me years before to ask me to read for the position of news anchor, the first on a Wichita station. I declined for it would be in conflict with Dick's position as business editor at The Eagle, and the salary did not measure up to my current pay. It also meant I would be walking away from a 15-year investment in my retirement program.

After we finished a Public Service program on KSOF,

Paul said, you should have taken my offer, you would have had no problem with the read and you look great in front of the camera. And he added, "You could have made history in this city – but I guess you've already done that." Nice that he thought I had.

The station was sponsoring a package trip to London with airfare, hotel and three shows included. It was the week after Thanksgiving, an offer we could not refuse. What a grand trip we had with 40 friends going on day trips, to shows and great meals. I went with Jerry and Paul Threlfall on a tour of Windsor Castle. The Queen was in residence and Paul spied her looking out the window at the Irish Changing of the Guard. Paul set his complicated professional camera and I took a picture of the two of them.

It turned out great and they used it on what was to be their last Christmas card. Jerry died shortly after the trip. Paul remarried but kept in contact with me until his death. Always a friend, always a mentor, always super supporter of me.

And speaking of supporters, another that had an important impact on my career was Paul Dannelley. One of the organizers of the Public Relations Society of Wichita, officer with a major advertising agency and then professor in the School of Journalism at the University of Oklahoma. I could count on him sending at least five students to Wichita each spring to interview me for job leads in the area. Some were hired here.

Don Granger continued close contact by phone, lunches and community projects. He was always available to mentor, counsel, inform, and be a protector. For years we celebrated his birthday, which was the same day as Grandpa Craig's in January, and mine in July.

How fortunate I have been to have had professional relationships with friends who cared about my career, liked Dick and enjoyed being with us socially.

After the holidays, I had a call from Rives asking me if I would be interested in responding to the request from the Convention and Visitors Bureau to be a loaned executive and work with them on the Miss USA Pageant to be held in Wichita in February. Yes, I would, for it would be an international telecast on CBS to more than 30 million people. What a great opportunity for Wichita, and for me.

The CVB president, Joe Boyd, said they needed someone to direct efforts by the news media for coverage. The pageant staff would take care of national and international contacts. On the spot, I became News Bureau Manager for the event and started working the next week in the media center.

The task was not only to manage local news, but also to fill requests from hometown media of the contestants. Some came with long lists, others none. We worked with local TV stations to contract with out-of-town stations for in-studio interviews.

Dick Clark and Leeza Gibbons arrived the week before the telecast, gave some local interviews but were protected by the pageant staff.

It was a position I would have for the next four years the pageant was held in Wichita. I also consulted with the CVB staff in 1995 when the Miss Teen USA pageant was held here.

It could have been a major annual event for the city but industry, business, community and civic leaders thought the international recognition had peaked, and they collectively were not interested in continuing raising the advance money to make it possible. The pros and cons were still being debated when, in later years, Donald Trump bought the pageant rights and Las Vegas became the selected city.

Dick Clark's wife, Karen, was usually with him and spent time in the media center with me. Clark and Gibbons used my desk and phone for their headquarters at Century II and would leave me fun notes for stories they thought were worth passing on to hometown papers. They could keep me busy without the 10- to 16-hour days of processing requests.

Wichita was gaining more publicity nationally through the pageant than any other event ever sponsored. A problem came up with animal rights activists demonstrating at entrances the night of the telecast. When I heard what was planned, I called the CVB, Boyd called city officials, and we received an order that they were not to come within 100 yards of the building for security reasons. They were protesting the delegates wearing fur coats, a gift most of them received from their state sponsors.

There are great stories over the span of four years. Nothing like looking up from my desk, seeing Olympic star Nadia Comaneci asking, "Do you know where I'm supposed to be?" Luckily I had the daily schedule of events and places handy. She sat on my desk while I gave her directions.

A surprising turn of events was with one of the celebrity judges, Charlie Pride. Even in winter he had his golf clubs with him so he could play at Terradyne, the golf-hotel complex where all the judges were staying.

His good friend Mike Oatman from the nationally recognized country music station, KFDI, called wanting an interview. Charlie said yes and I set up an interview at the hotel. It didn't happen there. Mike sent a limo to pick up Charlie at the hotel and before he knew it they were pulling into KAKE TV. He was escorted to the studio where Mike was already on air. He called to Charlie and he had no choice but to do a live interview. Mike pulled a fast one on both of us.

Charlie was not happy; he usually got paid for TV interviews. That evening when we were in the Celebrity buffet line at Century II, Charlie saw me and headed my direction. His wife stopped him and said, you leave that little girl alone, it was Mike, not her, that has you upset. I welcomed the interference and it made a believer of me that most of the "stars" need a traveling manager, and usually better if it is the wife.

During the year I had been the liaison with Craig Miner, a history professor and local book author, to set up interviews for the history he was writing about the Wolf Creek Generating Station. One of our trips to the plant, Craig made the comment that he had yet to write a book that the company stayed in business. I commented that because of Wolf Creek's indebtedness, I thought we were safe from a buy out.

During the interviews with the former CEOs and VPs, I learned more about strategic details than I had known during the construction time when I was giving so many public programs.

The "Amazing People" programs were all put back until spring so speeches came almost daily. In the summer I met with representatives from Enterprise for Education headquartered in Santa Monica, California. They had excellent energy education printed classroom material utilities that could be purchased for less than could be produced and printed locally. I told Glenn Craig that I was not in a position to contact other utilities to help market the material, but would recommend two programs be purchased for KG&E use.

The next day, Kansas City Power and Light, headquartered in Kansas City, Missouri, made a hostile offer to purchase KG&E. They were equal partners in two of the major electric generating facilities and would need all the excess power for their larger service and industrial base. The handwriting was bold and clear.

And, darn, Miner was right – he didn't have the book completed and we were on the sale block. The fight began.

Within three months, a merger had been struck with

the Topeka based utility for Kansas Power and Light and KG&E to join forces, eliminating the KCPL offer. General offices and staff would be moved to Topeka.

In November, anyone over 55 and with 20 years of service with the company was offered a retirement package. They added five years to our retirement package and would pay us a week salary for each year of employment. And they would cover our medical insurance until we reached age 65.

Dick and I talked about what my position would be with the company if I didn't take the offer. I learned I would be transferred to Topeka. Dick knew the KPL Corporate contact in Topeka and couldn't see me working with him. I then had a call from a good friend who was active with me in Kansas Press Women cautioning me that a move to KPL would probably not be a pleasant one for the same reasons Dick had outlined.

I took the retirement package but contracted back as a consultant with the company for the next year to complete my "Amazing People" commitments. With that time included, I worked 25 years and three days for KG&E.

How fortunate I had been to have so many opportunities with a respectable company. I began as an Advertising/Marketing Specialist and ended as Corporate Communication Administrator.

It was a great ride, and a springboard to many exciting opportunities that kept my "zest for living" on track at a high speed for a number of years after taking early retirement.

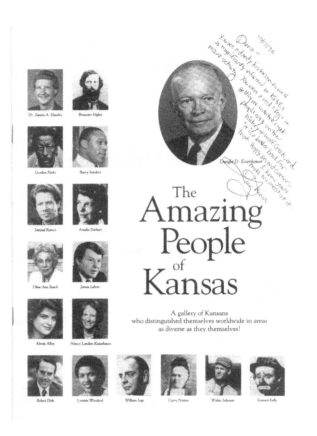

Amazing People of Kansas was developed into a speech, "Lou, Me and Katie" presented to civic organizations throughout the service area.

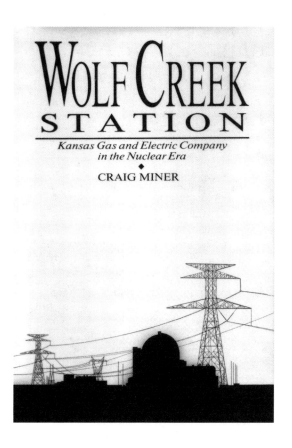

Liaison for Craig Miner who wrote a book on the history of Wolf Creek. His autograph on the opposite page reads:

"Donna -

> You are a dandy historian as well as magnificently informed on KG&E's recent activity. You were real 'key' in getting me with the right people early on the history of Wolf Creek and it is a better book for that. Happy second career, I know you'll make the most of it.
> - Craig Miner"

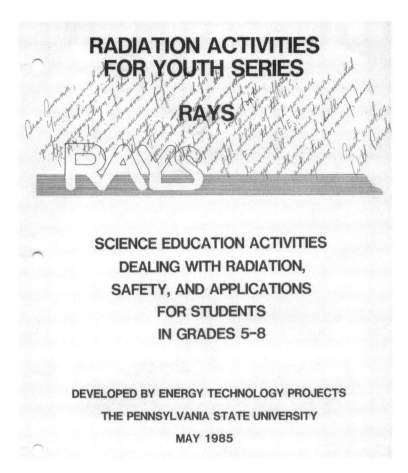

"Dear Donna, Your personal and professional input into the preparation of this RAYS book was surely the main reason it has been so successful as a key response for nuclear education.

"Thanks so much for your valuable work on the project and so many others that have had such an important impact on the energy education efforts of the utilities of the U.S."

Best wishes,
Walt Purdy (1991)

Edison Electric Institute
Washington, D.C.

Arriving as a VIP and chairman of the 1964 Wichita Press Women's Annual Beaux Arts Ball.

Louise Chaddic, Idaho, president of the National Federation of Press Women, joins me to watch a TV newscast in the Press Room at the 1968 National Conference held in Wichita.

Kansas Press Women award to Sue Hinkey.

Dilsaver Garners KPW Awards

Kansas Press Women each year honors members who have made outstanding contributions in several categories.

Donna Dilsaver, communications specialist in information services, won three awards in three separate categories for 1981.

Dilsaver won first place in the television category for producing a four-part series "Jobs in Energy." The series was aired on KPTS Channel 8 in the Wichita area and was produced for Women in Energy.

She also won a first place award in the media and other promotion category for coordinating a high school energy symposium on National Energy Education Day. The symposium was sponsored by KG&E, the Kansas Association of Teachers of Science and Women in Energy.

The Program Services Catalog published by Dilsaver won third place in the catalog and publications category. The catalog lists all education and speakers bureau programs available from KG&E. The award-winning entry was printed in-house.

Dilsaver's first place entries will now be entered in a national competition.

Donna Dilsaver (left) a communications specialist in information services, won three awards in the 1981 Kansas Press Women communications contest. Here, Donnis Harness, president of KPW, presents the awards.

Marge Setter, NFPW, Woman of Achievement, 2000, Donna, 2001.

KANSAS
Donna Dilsaver

Donna Dilsaver is a pioneer in the communications field and for recognizing women in their profession. In addition to her professional accomplishments, she has long used her skills to advance numerous civic projects and agencies, including managing the Miss USA Pageant for four years. She founded Women in Energy and implemented several awards to recognize women for their professional achievement. Today she serves on the boards of Orpheum Performing Arts Center, Girl Scouts Wichita Convention Sports Foundation, Friends Council, United Way, Wichita Convention Four America All-Indian Museum.

Dilsaver launched her writing career at the female sports writer for the *Wichita Eagle*. She in public relations for the Wichita Area Girl Sco and Electric. A long-time member of NFPW's has distinguished herself as president and in nur In 1968, she organized and ran the first news bu convention.

One of two women honored by the National Federation of Press Women as Woman of Achievement, September 12, 2001, in Indianapolis, Indiana.

Donna Dilsaver...
COMMUNICATOR OF ACHIEVEMENT

Donna Dilsaver was named the 2001 KPW Communicator of Achievement at the KPW state conference on May 5 in Hutchinson.

Donna is a pioneer both in the communications field and in recognizing women in their profession.

In addition to her professional accomplishments, she has long used her skills to advance numerous civic projects and agencies, including managing the news bureau at the Miss USA Pageant for four years and serving as spokesperson for the Save the Orpheum historic theater.

She launched her writing career at the age of 15 as the first female sports writer for the *Wichita Eagle*. On most occasions, she was the only female in the press box.

But she proved herself with credible reporting, earning the respect of professionals both on and off the field.

It was those early years as a reporter that set the theme for her strong will and tenacity to succeed. From that point on, she emphatically forged on as a pioneer of positive change for all professionals.

In college, she changed her major from English to sociology because she "wanted to help change the world," a creed she maintains today, nearly half a century later.

She had a long career in public relations for the Wichita Area Girl Scouts and Kansas Gas and Electric. She founded Women in Energy and implemented several awards to recognize women for their professional achievements.

Today she serves on the boards of Orpheum Performing Art Centre, Girl Scout Alumni and Friends, Wichita Convention Sports Foundation, Friends University Alumni Council, United Way, Wichita Convention Foundation and Mid-America All-Indian Museum.

A long-time member of KPW, she organized and ran the first news bureau at the national convention.

– *Colleen Brink*
2001 COA Chair

With Governor Joan Finney after being named Woman of Achievement in Energy.

With Governor Bill Graves following a Kansas Professional Communicators meeting.

With Senator Nancy Kassebaum Baker at the 19th Amendment 85th Celebration.

Emerald ball with actor Robert Young.

United Way Sound-off Chairman, 23 consecutive years.

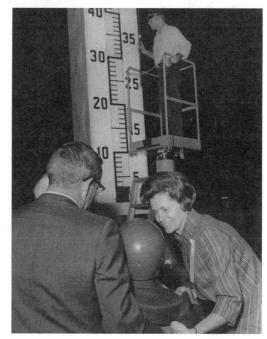

Named Wichita Woman 1999

Cover Story — **Donna Dilsaver**

by Kate Watson

Donna Dilsaver makes things happen.

For years, many local professional women's organizations have been unable to bring nationally recognized speakers to address their membership. (Such speakers' schedules require large audiences.) Last year Dilsaver, working through the Forum for Executive Women, gathered seventeen organizations to hear Senator Nancy Landon Kassebaum. The audience was composed of 333 delegates and guests. The atmosphere was charged with the energy of dynamic, influential women working together for the first time to turn national insight into local action. When Senator Kassebaum suggested, "Lets make this an annual event," the room exploded in applause. *Wichita WOMEN Magazine* and The Forum accepted the invitation to be the annual co-sponsors. Dilsaver hints that this year's gathering, May 2, will be even more historically significant than the last.

With a striking appearance, stately posture and dynamic speaking style, Dilsaver commands attention and respect. Forks suspend in mid-air when she speaks at luncheons. Her presentation on the evolution of the Kansas woman, a dramatization, is spellbinding.

Dilsaver served on the steering committee for the Miss USA Pageant, co-chairing with Marj Setter the media/public relations committee. Always one step ahead, Dilsaver was often overheard telling the national coordinators, "That's already been arranged."

Her latest challenge was coordinating communications from the KG&E crisis center to the media during the recent tornado devastation in Harvey County. The man who pulled his dead grandson out of the debris was a KG&E

184

10. New Directions

I didn't have much time to think about my "retirement" for I left KG&E on Friday and Monday went to meet with the two principles owners of Enterprise for Education in Santa Monica, California.

We agreed on travel expenses, compensation, and who I would contact. Many of the people I knew from the Edison Electric Institute Education group. I would begin in the spring for many were within driving distance of Wichita. Day drives but more efficient than flying.

In February I was back at the News Bureau of the Miss USA Pageant, which took me into March. Dick Clark was back in rare form and made work pleasant during the long hours.

The weekend following the pageant, Marge brought Thelma from her visit in Kansas City to stay with us and have foot surgery. The first week seemed okay during her healing but she began complaining more about a stomach problem. Kathy was giving her medical shots and one evening Thelma asked about her pain. Kathy then told Dick and me it was not Thelma's stomach but her intestinal tract. She got weaker by the day. At the end of the second week she wanted to go home and thought she should go to swing-care at the Smith County Hospital for a few days until she got to feeling better.

Marge and Dick both made it to Kensington for the Easter weekend when they thought she would have surgery. That was not to be; Thelma died the day before Dick's birthday, April 2, 1991.

My two weeks of caring for her seemed to launch the beginning of my next occupation – that of a caregiver.

In the summer, I did some traveling with success for Enterprise for Education, including out of the area to Chicago, Philadelphia, and Atlantic City. Cleah was visiting Linda at Wheaton, Illinois, to spent some time with her. Then she went to be with Marcia in Voorhees, New Jersey and I visited her there. Philadelphia was just across the river. They accompanied me to Atlantic City so I could combine personal with the orders the company was receiving for materials. It was a good arrangement for me.

Grace had not been taking her medicine and Dad could not take care of her at the apartment. In June she went to stay for a few weeks at the nearby Masonic Home. I curtailed my travels and spent more time taking Dad to see her. Between Kenneth, Dick and I, he was able to visit her most days. In fact, he rather enjoyed the company of the residents.

Grace was failing and was hospitalized at Wesley Medical Center, where she died September 14. She was the third person I had been with at the moment of death – Mother, Thelma and now Grace. Each different, each quietly, each with a moment of finality that is breathtaking.

Cleah came back again for Thanksgiving, with Sue's daughter, Erin, because Marcia and Paul were bringing Justin to see Dad (Poppy). Dad was doing well alone at the apartment as long as I was there frequently to do the laundry and some cooking.

He spent most of the holiday time with us at the house.

In February I again had the News Bureau at the pageant. Since I was downtown, it was easy for me to pick up some lunch and take my break with him. Dick was in Topeka for the legislative session so I had flexible time.

I was at a Friends Alumni Council Easter Egg Hunt when I went over to see him for a late breakfast. He showed me his toe and said he guessed he'd burnt it on his electric blanket. He was at the house for Easter Sunday dinner so I had Kathy look at it. She told us to get him to the doctor. Before taking him back to the apartment, I took him on a long drive around Jabara Airport where he had lived as a young man and where Kenneth was born. We had a grand time.

I took him to the doctor the next day. They did an angioplasty on his leg to see what was causing the circulation problem. They burst an artery in the process. He lost his foot, the good one. By July, he'd lost the problem foot. He worked so hard at physical therapy at Larksfield's Health Care Center but could not manage to gain control of his legs for a prosthesis.

In June I had the Goddard Alumni Banquet to coordinate for I had been elected president of the association the year before. A trip to the library for a few headlines and a quickly written speech made quick work of the program. It was delightful to reconnect with high school friends, especially Faye and DeeDee. We had been such good friends as teenagers but life had taken us different directions. We have stay closely connected since.

Dad was as comfortable as he could be sitting in a wheelchair all day. I was with him daily during the seven months he lived at Larksfield Place.

A pretty fall day in October, I wrapped him well with blankets in his wheelchair and took him for a long walk to the lake. He asked if I weren't too tired, could I push him around the back side of the facility. He then said, I hope you never regret the time you spend with me. Since I was behind him I said, we have great fun and good memories, and silently let the tears flow.

By December the doctor told us he was declining and that physical therapy would no longer be needed. Kenneth and I looked at each other, realizing what we had just been told. My time with him was interrupted only by attending Steve and Nancy's wedding after Christmas. Dad wanted us to go for him. It was Raymond's son who needed our support.

Dad died January 5, 1993, as I cradled his head in my arms and Kathy held his hand. Kenneth and Cleah arrived in the snowstorm shortly thereafter. Another finality, they are coming too close.

Kenneth had the responsibility of taking care of Dad's business. By February, I was back for the fourth Miss USA Pageant and had mixed feelings about it being the last year and yet relieved to be back in action with Dick Clark and the pageant staff I had come to enjoy each year.

The CVB asked me to help put together a not-for-profit foundation to accept contributions to be used to sponsor events in Wichita. Within weeks, we were an organization and I became president. I would continue for the next 12 years and serve three times as president. We connected with the Wichita Sports Commission, which I served on for a year. The group has been renamed the Wichita Convention and Sports Foundation and sponsors many youth sports events for the city. I take some pride and gratification in the leadership I provided to grow the organization.

Women in Energy was able to continue because women were now being promoted into management positions in the energy industry. Several conferences in the early '90s kept me involved in meaningful ways.

It was not unusual to have a phone call from former Washington Governor Dixy Lee Ray. She was appointed by President Nixon as the first and only woman to serve as the chairman of the Atomic Energy Commission in 1973.

She had written two books, "Environmental Overkill" and "Trashing the Planet." The latter was published in 1990. In my last letter from her in February 1991, she was so excited about her book and speaking tour. Rush Limbaugh, the dynamic radio talk show host, was sponsoring her on a trip to Florida. She was almost giddy as she told me about her lush car and hotel accommodations.

She wanted to know the Enterprise for Education Series 90 was progressing and had ideas for me to pass along to the developers of the curriculum materials.

Her calls from Fox Run and "running on the road" gave us meaningful conversations, and frequent contacts gave our friendship a joy to remember. Our morning chats became fewer, her health declined and she died in January 1994. It took months for me not to expect a call from her.

At the Chicago Women in Energy Conference in 1992, a group of us gathered in the quietest corner of the hotel bar we could find for conversation and exchange of ideas for the organization. Hazel Rollins O'Leary was the Woman of Achievement in Energy recipient and we had fun joking about the fame of Mrs. O'Leary's cow that legend credited with setting the Chicago fire.

Hazel had an impressive background and at the time was executive vice president of Northern States Power Company.

Joining us was Kay Kelly Arnold, government affairs vice president of Entergy Corporation; Arkansas Power and Light, Little Rock, Arkansas, was part of the company's new mix.

Bill Clinton had just been nominated as the Democrat candidate for President. The conversation rotated to Hillary, who was an attorney friend of Kay's in Little Rock. With the new couple focusing on women in a variety of positions if elected, we started speculating on who some might be.

I turned to Hazel and said, "How about Secretary of Energy? You've had a lot of experience with government positions and now you're upper echelon of females in major utility companies. You could manage it." Kay said, "Why not? I hope to be on the Clinton transition team; maybe it can happen."

So, it was not a surprise to the speculating women. Hazel R. O'Leary was the first woman and the first black to be appointed to the cabinet position of Secretary of Energy, a position that was created with the department in 1980.

Today, Kay has a long list of accomplishments to her credit. Her husband, Richard, died in 1994. His credits were extensive and had he not been diagnosed with cancer, he would have been nominated by Clinton for Supreme Court of the USA.

When Kay graciously agreed to come to Wichita to speak to the Executive Forum for Women for me, Clinton had taken office. Many in our small conversation group had many questions about the first couple. I asked Kay how much she thought Hillary would be directly involved with government affairs. Her response was, "You better hope she is around close someplace for Bill can be like a loose cannon. She's the one who can keep him focused."

Some of my friends and I have since commented on how very accurately she assessed the situation with the Clintons.

Following a Board of Directors meeting in New York in February, we planned a meeting in the Northeast, shopping for a prestigious location but keeping costs under control. The Northeast chapter did us proud by scheduling it at West Point. What a delightful setting, attracting many speakers with impressive qualifications.

The Woman of Achievement in Energy was Dr. Gail De Planque, past president of the American Nuclear Society and nuclear scientist extraordinaire. She had long been a member of our organization but had not been in a position to accept the award prior to our being on the east coast.

When Chernobyl happened in 1986 at the flawed reactor-designed Russian Nuclear Power Plant in the Ukraine, Gail was one of the first three nuclear physicists sent from the United States to assess the damage. Unlike those built in the states, Russia did not build the massive buildings to contain any radiation that might escape from the facility.

No significant radiation-release from the facility

show any health effects through the 2006 study.

When a position opened on the Nuclear Regulatory Commission (NRC) there was no better qualified candidate available than Gail. Women in Energy and others in the nuclear industry began sending messages to President Clinton to appoint her.

Even though she was a Democrat, Clinton believed her to be too qualified with too much experience with the nuclear industry. His decline to appoint her was the beginning of his decline of our perception of him as a bright leader and an environmental activist.

This attitude and lack of insight to the future energy needs of this country brought to an even greater decline the construction of the much needed clean electricity that could be generated with nuclear fuel.

My role with the organization was changed from being with a nuclear utility company to an honorary position. One of the last meetings I attended was in St. Louis, Missouri, in 1995. So much of the industry had changed. If the utility was not being bought out or merged, it was in the buying mode.

Women were being promoted to key executive positions, accomplishing much of what Women in Energy's mission had been in the first place, communicating to women about energy issues. What these women had in common was hard work, intellect, a mile-high stack of education and the very strong will to do something to better their lives and that of others. With that focus, glass ceilings not only cracked, they shattered.

What an accomplishment for me to have been a significant part of helping that happen.

The word must have spread that I might be available for other volunteer tasks for soon my longtime friend, Marge Setter, president of Save the Orpheum Theatre, called to ask me to take over the radio and television management and appearances for the theatre. I began slowly, then found myself making radio spot announcements and frequent live television appearances to promote fund raising events.

The major and largest attended event was the showing of "Gone With the Wind" back on the big screen. We had a full page feature story in The Wichita Eagle, every radio and television station helped promoted the two-night showing, and we had record attendance at both.

Robert Osborne, the same person who introduces all the Turner Classic Movies with such flair, came to do the same for us opening night. We were guests on Gene Countryman's Kansas on KNSS radio in the morning. During the day he contacted Olivia de Haviland in Paris to tell her of the showing. She sent a message to us to the delight of the first-nighters.

I continued on the Orpheum Theatre Board of Directors in a public relations position until 2004 when they honored me with the position of Board Member Emeritus.

In 1994, I took over as owner/manager of the Lazy RB Ranch. I had promised Dad that I would try to keep as much of his 320-acre place together as I could. Kenneth and Betty decided to sell his 80 acres at the time of the closing of the estate. I purchased Raymond's children's 80 acres when they decided that none of them were in a position to take over the management. I did not want the responsibility of doing it for them.

If I could have the place for 15 years, I thought there were things that needed to be done to improve the production. I bought a small Class-C motor home to have to stay in and created an area near the barn to park it. Then I worked with the Soil Conservation District to begin the improvements. First we dug a major pasture pond in the northwest 80. The contractor hit an artesian well, assuring water would be available to cattle most of the time. I made arrangements for almost a mile of shelterbelt to be planted along the north side to provide shelter for deer and hold moisture.

I continued the rental contract that Kenneth had established with Glen Fieser.

Legal assistance for ranch concerns came from Willard (Bill) Thompson and former Kansas Senator Bob Wunsch of Kingman.

In the next 10 years I grew the ranch from the 80-acres I inherited from Dad and Mother to include the 320 acres of the original family ranch, and the Vic Callahan 160 acres connecting to the west bounded by the Chikaskia River. The total 480 acres is gradually being turned over to Ron to manage and eventually own. If he keeps it there will be 160 acres for each of his children. Dad taught me never to spend the land of the next generation. So far, I have been able to hold true to his teachings.

During the last 15 years of my employment, I was able to save, invest and realize enough money to purchase the ranch, build the Santa Fe style house, improve the pastures with a pond in each, build a mile of shelterbelt, build and maintain miles of fences. What little I inherited from family was invested in the ranch on my own. It is an accomplishment I reflect upon with satisfaction.

In May I ran into a health problem and had surgery. I took it easy for the next two months to be certain the mesh installed to hold my bladder in place was secure.

We had moved Dick's Uncle Oliver from Boulder, Colorado, to Larksfield Place in 2002. I had taken care of him during Dad's stay and continued to visit him at least three times a week. Frequently I had Danny and took him with me. Uncle Oliver had lost two children when they were very young and had latched on to "the boy" with hugs each time he saw him. The two became great friends. He could not remember my name so called me "the pretty one." Not a bad name, always flattered me.

Dick was working full time at Coleman; I kept up my

volunteer projects and the ranch.

I had told Danny to think about where he wanted to go next year on his 10-year trip. He wanted to go a year early for he was "old for his age." I had told him anyplace in the United States; he decided Alaska. Katie and Kristen didn't think that was fair – that I should have said the continental U.S.

Since traveling alone with a boy is more difficult, we asked Dick to join us. What a grand wildlife trip we had to Denali National Park, Fairbanks to see the Ox, Art Museums with Chihuly glass displays, and on to Seward for a boat ride to watch the whales. It was an unforgettable experience for each of us.

At the time of Thelma's death, Dick had promised Jo we would come see her in Australia in the next five years. Marge had been there in the winter. By September, Jo and Tom had nearly completed their country home so Dick decided we should go.

We toured Charley's Creek area then the four of us went to Darwin to visit Peter, their son, who was stationed there in the Navy. We had a great time in Kaka do National Park and other sights. Tom went home, and Jo, Dick and I went to Alice Springs, Ayres Rock and then to Perth. A grand tour of the continent.

We had three days on Fiji Island before coming home, which was pleasant, but not exciting.

Part of my problem throughout the trip was I had abdominal pains that would not be relieved in any position or activity. I was ever so relieved to be home and went to two doctors. They suggested exploratory surgery. At Ed Moore's insistence, we checked to see if I could go to Mayo Clinic for a second opinion.

Finally arrangements were made for me to go in December. Dr. Stanhope took one look at the X-rays I had with me, asked his nurse if second surgery was open in the morning. It was and I went under his knife early the next day. He took out all the mesh net that had come loose and was floating in my abdominal area. He said, "No wonder you hurt." I stayed under their care for five days.

That is when I became aware that Dick was having memory problems. He was having problems getting from the hotel to my room at the hospital. I noticed it the year before but thought it to be pressure at work and with Lee's health problems with Crohn's.

We came home and I took the winter off to recuperate while Dick went to Topeka for the legislative session.

One trip he wanted to make was to see his childhood friends and their wives, Kent and Betty Carroll in North Carolina and Bud and Sue Bierman in Florida. I had seen Dick excited about a trip before but this was different. He was becoming increasingly aware of his thinking processing problems, as was I.

We went to the Carrolls first, and Dick was so very pleased to see them. We spent two nights in their home on the golf course in Pinehurst. Betty prepared a delicious beef dinner for us the first night, the second we went to the Country Club of North Carolina, a special place to them and a treat for us. During the day, Kent took us through the area of Weymouth Woods Sandhill Nature Preserve and about 30 miles to Fort Bragg on a grand tour.

Kent drove the four of us to Florida giving a running dialogue of what we were seeing most of the way. Sue and Bud had a cook-out prepared for us when we arrived. During the next day Kent and Bud played golf; Dick walked with them and enjoyed every moment.

Sue, Betty and I went shopping at a very large mall. It was a first for me – I had never gone shopping in a mall with friends. The discount store had many name brands and Betty was an exceptional shopper. She spied a dark turquoise silk pant suit on a mannequin and said, you would look smashing in that, perfect for an informal dinner at the club. Then she found a white pant suit for me, perfect for sailing, she said. I purchased both and have worn the silk suit many times, but the white suit hangs in a bag for when and if I ever go sailing. It was an exceptional day for me.

The Carrolls drove us to our next stop, Disney World and Epcot Center. I can still see Betty's face in the car window, waving and saying, "Let's do this again."

I commented to Dick, as we entered our hotel room, what a delightful couple Kent and Betty were and what gracious hosts they had been. Dick agreed, then said of his dear friend:

"Vice Admiral Kent Carroll is as perfect a man as you will ever know."

We finished our trip and over the years Dick kept a picture of the three – him, Kent and Bud in his study. It remains there today.

In 1997 Dick was wrapping up his time with the Coleman Company as he turned 70 in April. It was increasingly apparent that Dick was having major memory problems. I had gone to Topeka with him several times for he was lost coming once and that was enough. I drove him there several times.

Our granddaughters had classmates go with them to page in the House of Representatives several times so my being with Dick was not unusual. A number of times I stopped by Governor Bill Grave's office to give him a personal message from a mutual friend.

By the time Jo and Jenny came to visit in May, Dick was unable to make plans for their time and asked many questions about common knowledge. Following their visit in June, Dick was officially diagnosed with Alzheimer's by three doctors.

To keep him active and us together, I traded the small RV for one I had liked from Bob and Amy Feldner. I could park it at the ranch, stay there, or we could be out on the road.

Having the opportunity to be at the ranch and seeing how it could be so much more, I contacted the U.S. Soil Conservation office. They began planning and making suggestions for improvements. We planted almost a mile of shelterbelt along the north side of the pastures, built a 12-foot pasture pond in the otherwise dry north pasture. The effort gained the ranch the coveted Shelterbelt Conservation Award for Kingman County in 1997.

I'd just come in from a cold stay at the ranch when Dad's cousin, Ralph Nair, in California called to say he had made contact with Grandma Bolton's family in Prague, Czech Republic, but could not go to see them. It was a natural for me. We began with his University of California friends from Prague with conference calls to Helena.

In October, I went to meet Helena and Joseph in Prague. Dick would come a week later to meet me in London. By then he had been diagnosed with Alzheimer's but was still functioning well for daily tasks and driving. Every step of the trip was arranged and inprint for him by a very capable travel agent. It worked well. I was at the hotel one hour after his arrival.

We took the rest of the month to tour South Ireland, a circle of Scotland and some unique time in London. A day trip I planned in England was a bus trip to the White Cliffs of Dover, a place Dick had always wanted to see. What a great trip and he remembered none of it within months after we arrived home.

At lunch with a longtime friend from Press Women, Eleanor Mayne asked what I was doing for myself. I told her I was trying to keep my sanity while keeping up with daily business and medical concerns. Then she suggested I begin making notes of my career and the people who helped me along the way. She said, "You should write a book, for young women will not know what it was like to be a 'first' as you have been so many times and what it is like to rear a family and have a highly responsible professional career."

We laughed and thought a good title would be "A View From Under The Glass Ceiling." Then corrected ourselves for I'd had the opportunity to look down from above shattered ones.

Dick liked checking his e-mail. So many friends were gracious and kept in close contact with him with frequent notes. He delighted in the jokes sent to him by childhood friend Bud and Sue Bierman. I don't think Bud knew I was reading some of them to him. Others kept him informed on what was happening in Topeka. Kent Carroll kept short but interesting notes coming and was supportive of us both.

Dick was able to drive his Jeep around town until 1999. I became aware that if he were to live out of a care facility as long as possible, the townhouse Kathy's parents had lived in at the time of their deaths would be much safer for him and more manageable for me.

We took trips in the RV to Tucson, Arizona, to be with cousins Ross and Alberta and with Bob and Amy who were wintering there. We went to Lutzen, Minnesota, on Lake Superior to once again visit Betty and Charlie Pearson. The next winter was to the east coast to Savannah, Georgia, to tour with Bob and Amy Feldner.

On the last trip I asked Dick if he wanted to drive up to see his friends the Carrolls. He said no, he didn't want Kent to see him in his condition. We came home, the last of our major trips in the motor home. He had never learned to drive it.

We continued to spend some time at the ranch but Dick was not enjoying being away from busy work in his den and contact with friends on the computer.

In the spring of 2000, I sold the motor home, sold our home of 24 years on Stratford, purchased and moved into the townhouse.

Marge Setter and I are included in initial Plaza of Heroines at Wichita State University.

Robert Osborne on KNSS promoting "Gone With the Wind" at the Orpheum.

Named Board Member Emeritus for the Orpheum Theatre.

Bonnie Bing/The Wichita Eagle

The star of the evening was the vestibule floor at the Orpheum Theatre. Special guests checked out the new floor, heard about progress on the renovation from Orpheum president Mary Eves and watched the 1940s documentary about our city, "Wings Over Wichita." Among those attending the cocktail buffet were longtime supporters Mary and Delmar Klocke, Donna Dilsaver and Marge Setter.

a. Katie's 10th birthday trip to California, 1989.
b. Kristen's 10th birthday trip to Florida, 1993.
c. Belated trip with Laura to see Six Flags over Texas, 1995.

Ron's family to Hawaii, Dick and I to Australia, 1995.

Kristen and I went to see Laura in Joffrey Ballet, New York City.

Danny's 9th birthday trip with Dick and me to Alaska, 1995.

Katie, high school, Kristen's 8th grade graduation trip to Alaska, 1997.

a. & b. Katie, college, Kristen, high school, Danny, 8th grade, Tahiti, Moorea, 2001.

c. Katie, master's degree, Kristen, college, Danny, high school, family cruise to Caribbean, 2005.

New Directions:
Ranch Growth from 80 acres to 480 acres

a. Poppy with Ron, Katie, Kristen and Danny at Ranch.

b. Soil Conservation Award, Dick and Rancher Glen Fieser attend.

c. Planting 1-mile shelterbelt.

Kathy with Bandit.

Danny, Kristen, Kathy, Ron.

Ron at the Chickaskia River.

With cousins, Wesley and Beth, Aunt Mildred Shannon, Aunt Billie and Uncle Steve.

At the ranch, Dick with Phil and Connie Dietz, Robin and Eric McGonigle.

Donna and Dick with his sister, Jo.

Bill and Joean Calhoun, Dick, Betty and Charlie Pearson.

Parkhursts with us at the ranch.

Dick's Jellyneck group.

Kent Carroll at the ranch.

Ranch Neighbors

Glen and Debby Fieser.

Sig and Charles Rhodes.

RVing with Amy and Bob Feldner, Arizona to Georgia.

a. Trip to North Carolina to visit Dick's Kensington childhood friends, Dick, Kent and Bud, October 1996.
b. Dick, me, Sue and Bud Bierman.
c. Dick, me, Betty, Vice Admiral Kent Carroll.

a. Later years, visit with Betty and Jean Stiles.
b. Donna, Faye and DeeDee.
c. At the Pacific Ocean with Kenneth.

Apple Butter Day at Raynor's in Marshall, Missouri.

Veteran's Day, Dick's Memorial at Kensington with Marge.

Betty and Kenneth in my home.

Last picture with all four siblings, 1982.

We three with Dad and Grace at Friends Village.

Cleah, with family, Ed, Sue, Linda, Marcia, Donald.

a. Kenneth with David's family.
b. Phyllis and Raymond's family. (Raymond is deceased.)
c. Erin & Andrew's wedding with Sue & Marcia.

David, Paul and Kenneth.

Celebrations with Bolton cousins.

With cousins, Joseph and Helena Vignati Anton and Michal.

11. Care Giving, a Rewarding Choice

Dick's Den at the townhouse was as near like it had always been as I could arrange it. With the same sofa and a new television set we spent many evenings in the small room while the downstairs was converted from storage space to a spacious family room, bathroom and office for me.

Aunt Mildred, mother's 90-year-old sister, ran into health problems and could not stay in her home. She was moved to a care facility and I began spending time caring for her. Dick and she loved to visit so being there made it easier for me. Danny began spending time with her after school and was a great help in taking some of the load off my time.

Since Dick could not be left home alone, he was with me most of the time. His friends from more than 30 years in AA promised me that they would see us through Dick's Alzheimer's, regardless of how much time it took.

They were faithful to their word. They picked him up for their traditional Thursday lunch, Wednesday evenings, and I joined them for dinner each Friday night. What great friends and what a sacrifice to make such a commitment to the two of us.

In the fall of 2000 I contracted with a builder to construct a small 1,200 square foot house at the ranch so we could be there. By the end of 2001 we were spending a lot of time and having visitors come for a meal. I didn't need to worry about Dick wandering away from the paddock and I could relax in the hot tub and enjoy the serenity of a Kansas sunset.

In June, after Katie had graduated from college, Kristen from high school and Danny from the 8th grade, I took them on a graduation trip to Tahiti and Moorea Islands while Kathy and Ron took care of Dick at home. It may have been a sanity saver for me. We had a real island experience, a major respite for me.

I was about packed, had food prepared for easy servings, and was preparing to leave for Indianapolis for the National Federation of Press Women's national convention. I was one of two women to be awarded the coveted national Woman of Achievement designation. This honor from my peers was immensely important to me for it validated my long career in communication and public relations work.

As I returned home from having Holly style my hair, she called and told me to turn on the TV to see the news. Dick was in his Den with the TV on and I saw what was the second airplane crash into the World Trade Center. It was the morning of September 11, 2001. As I watched the unfolding national news with astonishment, I knew quick changes needed to be made.

I called the airlines and was amazed to get through immediately to cancel my plane reservations for the next day. Then I called the hotel to learn that many attendees were already there and the convention would go on as planned, but I cancelled.

As I hung up, a call came from the national Achievement chairman in Washington, D.C. Her husband was at the Pentagon and she was calling me on the land phone leaving the cell for him to contact her. She had been ready to drive to Indianapolis when the crash happened. She wanted me to stay with her until she heard from her husband so I could make some calls for her. The lines were being tied up there.

Finally after more than a half-hour, her husband called to say he was on his way home, safe, and that she should plan on leaving for the convention as planned.

Of all that happened that day, I could not feel sorry for myself that I would not be present to acknowledge the honor. A few weeks later when the gold engraved discs arrived I did feel saddened, not for me, but for the nation and what had prevented me from receiving them firsthand at a banquet with my peers, not in a padded package.

My life could go back on track. I so hoped President Bush would take appropriate action. Others had not when we had been attacked before.

Living with an Alzheimer's patient is a lonely life. Without friends giving support, love and a hug, it can be almost unbearable. That's why, when we had a note from Kent Carroll that Betty was suffering from the same ailment, I knew what they were facing, and to a degree, so did Dick.

He had me re-read Kent's e-mail and asked why this had to happen, we could have taken another trip with them. They had invited us to join them in Bali.

I started taking Dick to day care at the Center for Living. By November, I knew full well that I could not take care of Dick in our home much longer. He had my arm in his very strong hands and was trying to break it in two. I kissed him on the forehead and told him he was hurting me. He finally realized what he was doing and stopped, only to look at me with a blank stare.

I promised myself I would make it through the holidays and give our grandchildren one last Christmas with him at home. On January 16, 2003, Raymond's birthday, Dick went to live in a care facility, never to return to the townhouse or the ranch.

After a kidney stone surgery, he no longer qualified for the lovely facility where I'd set up a small apartment for him. The day I was moving him to the Catholic Care Center was the day of his son Elmer Lee's funeral in Topeka. Ron and Kathy attended, I could not. We never told Dick about Elmer Lee's death of Crohn's disease.

In March, Kenneth and I took a long weekend to Fresno, California, to see his son Paul in the Captain's role in "The Sound of Music." It was good for me to have a break and know all could go well for Dick with me not present every day.

Laura, Debra's daughter, had been selected for a summer program with Joffrey Ballet in New York City. I had told her if she ever made it to a NYC stage, I would be there. Ron and Kathy offered again to help with Dick, and Kristen was available to accompany me to the Big Apple.

In addition to seeing Laura perform, we attended two Broadway shows, "Rent" and "42nd Street." Laura joined us for the latter. Kristen and I took the subway to Ground Zero, saw the plans for the future, and agreed that we should return when it is completed. I hope it is completed in my lifetime.

At the same time, I tried to spend as much time with Kenneth and the boys as I could. He was caring for Betty at home with many trips to the doctors and stays in the hospital. After a stay in early September, they gave her no hope but only days for her life. She died just before they were to celebrate their 50th wedding anniversary, her services were held on that day. Fifty red roses draped her casket and at the closing, Kenneth gave each woman at the cemetery a flower to help him celebrate the day with Betty.

One day I saw a picture of an old stone house, half of it wasted to the weather. I was reminded of a fine stone house next to the highway on our many trips to Kensington to visit Dick's parents. One Memorial Day weekend there were many cars in the farmyard, obviously a funeral service had taken place.

As the years passed, it was obvious no one lived there. The life, the spirit, the very soul was gone. Gradually the house diminished until the last storm took what had been away. Vanished, what was, was no more. The land was bare. Only memories linger.

I thought to myself, that's what is happening to Dick. His life, his spirit, his very soul is gone. One day all will vanish and a final storm will take him away just as it did the house. The thoughts made me sad, but at the same time gave me some peace of mind that God's will, certainly not mine, was in control.

I visited him daily, took care of his clothes and ambled through the days for 18 months. The last two weeks of his life I stayed in the same room with him. His strong heart would not give out while he wasted away. I played his favorite WWII music using four long-playing cassettes. Ron and Kathy thought he would depart on the song, "When the Saints Go Marching In."

On Wednesday morning, August 4, 2004, at 7:45 as the song "I'll Never Smile Again Until I Smile at You" was playing, Dick died.

As he had requested, a Communion and Visitation service was held Saturday night at Pine Valley Christian Church and a service to dedicate what was being established as a memorial, bronze sculptured turkeys, was held at the Great Plains Nature Center. His service was on Kenneth's birthday, August 8.

Years before, he had made notes of those he wanted to speak at his services: Ed Moore, Charlie Pearson, Kent Carroll, Charlie McIlwaine. Ed was available, Charlie was at the lake, McIlwaine was in Colorado and Kent was taking care of Betty at home in North Carolina.

For the most part, his services were as he had wanted. His ashes are buried by our marker at Jamesburg Cemetery, 1700 North Tyler in Wichita. He had lived most of his life here with me. A few of his ashes are with his military marker at Germantown Cemetery with his parents in Kensington's countryside.

I shall always cherish and return his love, blessed by this gentle loving, devoted husband of 43 years.

222

12. Adjustment, with Support from Family and Friends

I busied myself in planning for the unveiling of the bronze turkey sculpture display at the Great Plains Nature Center in mid-October. The event was mostly arranged by Bob Gress with my suggestions and guest list. Larry Jones would be a speaker, that was quickly confirmed. I invited Kent to do the same if he could possibly get away. He could not, but would certainly try to come this way to visit the center when he could. The dedication of the Turkey Memorial, "Through the Woods," was held during the Art on the Trail Day at the Great Plains Nature Center in October. Larry Jones was the speaker.

It meant that Ron and Kathy could not be here for they had Parent's Day at Pepperdine with Danny. However, it was possible for Marge, Debra and Laura to be there. The Praise Band from Pine Valley Christian Church agreed to play. Never have turkeys been so beautifully serenaded.

It was a lovely fall day, perfect weather. Laura pulled the fabric from the single turkey, Debra from the two hens, and Marge and I unveiled the large Tom. They stand at the entrance to the GPNC. A memorial to Dick and a tribute to all those who have made the wild life center a major attraction in the state.

I have the bronze table model of the birds in the living room. They not only are a tribute to Dick, but a reminder of days we honored his memory.

It would have meant so much to Dick, as it did to me, to have Kent pass this way on a trip to visit the center and the ranch. He now knew where Dick and I spent much of our last time together.

I continued to go to the Alzheimer's Support Group I'd helped start and was appointed to the Leadership Council of the Alzheimer's Association. I was giving time to support some friends who were caregivers, including our longtime friends Carl and Gwen Bell. She had been Senator Kassebaum's administrative assistant and my close friend. She later died of cancer. She just wore herself out in his care.

When asked at a support group meeting how they had heard of the meeting, several, including Gwen, said that I insisted they begin attending. Paul Wilson, a longtime friend from the Wichita Advertising Club whose wife had Alzheimer's, turned and said, "Donna, of all the accomplishments I know you have achieved in your career, none can match the valuable gift you give in support of caregivers of those with Alzheimer's. We thank you with gratitude and affection." It was one of the most meaningful tributes I have received.

It took me seven months to sort through 62 file boxes Dick had stacked in his office, downstairs and even in the barn at the ranch. Most, at one time, were in order but during the last years of his "office" work, every file was mixed beyond recognition of title.

I completed the task and had filed all the tax information and taken care of all of his trust work, including distributing to family and friends items as he directed.

All of his close friends who had given me support, friendship and love were continually calling, inviting me to join them or assuring me that life would get better.

Dick's hunting buddy and close friend Ed Moore had been diagnosed with cancer, had surgery, treatments and was very ill in weeks shortly after Dick's death. We visited almost nightly on the phone, just checking in he'd say. Or, when are we going for that steak dinner? Knowing full well, that was not remotely possible.

After Christmas, matters worsened with Ed. My longtime friend Betty Tumlinson was in the hospital with a heart ailment and my neighbor Norma died suddenly with bronchial problems. Betty soon followed and it became increasingly evident that Ed was not going to make it.

At about my lowest point, Cleah and I talked about her unhappy home situation and I suggested she come back to Kansas to spend her 77th birthday with us. It was arranged but for some reason she booked herself into Kansas City in place of Wichita. She was more confused than I'd realized.

Kenneth and I drove to Kansas City in the evening to meet her, spent the night at a motel and drove to Wichita the next day. She was so happy to see us, which lifted my spirits. After a day's rest we would decide how to spend the two weeks she would have with us.

I sent an e-mail to many friends and family to let them know she was visiting. I made arrangements for me to be online less and plan to share time with them, alerting them to her apparent beginning dementia problems. After she was settled in for the night, I went upstairs to do the same.

As I entered the room, the phone rang and the caller said, "This is Kent Carroll, I'll bet you're surprised to hear from me." Yes, I said, but pleased. He asked many questions about Cleah's dementia condition, and then told me of Betty's declining health with Alzheimer's. She had not known him since 2003. He asked if he could continue to stay in contact, he appreciated the way I took care of Dick and my experience with Alzheimer's. He wasn't getting much information from doctors.

A flood of memories came back of how Dick's friends had been so helpful to me, and as I dropped off to sleep, I made the same commitment to Kent and Betty to see them through the journey to the end. It began March 10, 2005, as I drifted of to sleep.

In the morning, Cleah and I made plans for activities and making arrangements to be with family. We joined Kenneth and Jane for a Singing Quaker's program, went to movies, visited friends, had family gatherings including spending time in Lyons with Phyllis, Phil, Steve and Nancy – to celebrate the twins' birthday. And, she rested. It was one of the best visits we had shared in years. It was her last trip to Kansas and I was determined to have her enjoy it to the fullest and leave happy. She did.

In the middle of April, Ed Moore died. He had been a dear friend to Dick and me. He died too young and suffered too long in the process. Too many of our friends were dying. I was spending a lot of time at the ranch and one evening decided I needed to spend more time with friends and not continue to be as isolated as I was during Dick's long illness.

Don Tanner, another hunting buddy, would stop by for coffee while his wife, Irene, shopped at Towne East. They have not been in good health for some time and I try to stay in contact with them.

Betty and Charlie Pearson have come to dinner several times before leaving to spend the summer at their lake home.

Beverly Hoover and I filled mornings at the Y working out and doing whatever comes on the social calendar, sometimes even just a movie.

There is no doubt, this was a wandering time, trying to focus on meaningful things to keep life interesting and to be a vital, happy person. Keeping that zest for life that Dick wanted me to keep was becoming more vague.

Kent, thankfully, was true to his word and began sending me the most interesting e-mail from his military buddies as well as asking questions and giving me updates on Betty's progressive problems as they coped with Alzheimer's. To put him on the same page with me, I sent him a copy of the booklet from the Mayo Clinic on Alzheimer's disease.

He also asked if I might still have a copy of the first chapter of the book he was writing that he had once sent to Dick. Yes, it was still in the very large file folder marked in large black letters, "Kent." He asked if I would take a look at it and give him any ideas. In a few days I received a large packet with the first chapters. Because Dick kept him so close, it was easy for me to continue.

In May, Kristen graduated from Rockhurst College, Danny from Independent High School and we had not had a chance to celebrate Katie's master's degree graduation. I decided it would be fun for the family to take one last trip together – my first cruise and trip to the Caribbean. Kathy is an excellent tour planner so I turned all the arrangements over to her. She did well. We were gone for nine days, seven aboard a Carnival ship.

We toured Puerto Rico, Dominica Republic, Barbados with the last Aruba. A college girl, Natalee Holloway, was reported missing and a major search effort was underway. Kristen, Danny and I jetted out to a small island to snorkel. A helicopter was circling above us as I swam a large roped off area just to be sure we were seeing only fish. As I reached near the ropes, I felt the tug of the ocean and quickly moved back toward the beach. It wouldn't take much to be swept out to sea. Kristen tanned while Danny and I swam with the big blue fish. It was delightful.

That night we went to the nightclubs, Carlos and Charlie's where Natalie had last been seen by friends. I asked Kristen what she would have done had that been Jen. She said she would have slapped the s--t out of the guy and sat on Jen so she couldn't leave. That was comforting for I thought Jen might do the same for Kristen.

It was no doubt that many under-age drinking American students go there for the right-of-passage. The town is designed and geared toward that age college group.

Our day-tours had been interesting and I enjoyed being on the water and cruise activities and night programs. We sailed overnight back to Puerto Rico for a night's stay before heading home. We visited the Bacardi Rum factory. There I had my first rum-and-coke, which the grandkids could not believe. But, the rum cake was not nearly as good as the one Beverly makes. She isn't slack on the rum.

We had a great time. When we got home and I had a chance to look at some of the pictures, I realized some things will happen only once, my grandchildren are growing up into lives of their own. Their time will be limited as mine becomes more free.

Dick's childhood friend Bud Bierman died, the second of the threesome from the Kensington childhood that Dick cherished. I try to keep up with Bud's wife, Sue. She now lives in an independent living facility near her daughter in Colorado.

More of my time was being spent keeping up with friends and family on the computer. Kent sent a note that Betty's agitation was increasing and he was considering better care for her in a very good facility nearby so he could visit her daily. That happened in 2005.

I spent as much time with Danny as possible for he was leaving to go to college at Pepperdine University in Santa Monica, California. Ron and Kathy would drive out and fly back. I was going to miss him so very much. Kristen was remaining in Kansas City to be close to Justin, and Katie was in Dallas, hardly available for a quick sandwich or a pizza dinner on the run.

There were changes I needed to make in my life. One was my continued attendance at Pine Valley Christian Church. My age group had grown smaller and those attending were not in good health. Longtime friend Beverly Hoover invited me to start attending Wednesday night dinners at the Cornerstone Cafe with study to follow at Eastminster Presbyterian Church. I did, and liked being back to the church of my youth. I attended the new members' class and joined the church by statement of faith. I still maintain a membership at PVCC and attend occasionally.

Mary and Bill Chesnut are also members as well as

many other longtime friends from scattered acquaintances of living in the same city.

Along with Mary, I kept up with friends from my days on the Girl Scout professional staff. I became a life member of Girl Scouts of the USA.

The Orpheum Theatre board made me a board member emeritus and I continue with events and staff working to restore the theatre to its days of glory of the 1920s.

A task I continued to enjoy was being president for the third time of the Convention Sports Foundation board. The one-cent sales tax funds were growing and in the next few years we should have a new Sports Complex to compliment the other convention facilities.

Wichita Professional Communicators monthly luncheons meetings are permanently on my schedule, and I rarely miss a meeting. That is where I see most of my professional friends. I am a life-member of the National Federation of Press Women and the Kansas Professional Communicators.

Serving on the Leadership Council for the Alzheimer's Association has taken up much of my volunteer time.

The Friday Night dinner group that Dick and I first attended in August, 1970, has changed to the point that I am the only original member. The group grew to be about eight couples, we've added people, and now shrank to about seven of us in good weather. Beverly continued to join us with Marty and Bill Rush, Holly and Bill Anderson being the small but loyal group. There were times life would have been empty without their support and friendship.

During most of the days, I stay in contact through e-mail to make arrangements with friends. As Kent and I carried on correspondence, we shared Kansas University basketball, men's and women's golf and other sports. Since I had read so much about him as I put editing marks in his book, he asked me to send him my bio and level the playing field. I e-mailed what has been sent to organizations or clubs when I was the speaker to be introduced.

He was impressed, saying he had been in the military and had not known many professional women with my background and experience. He thought I should do the same as he, write a book for my grandchildren so they would know more about my career. I told him I'd think about it. Eleanor had made the suggestion years ago as have other friends.

He asked me if I played golf. When I said no, he suggested I take some lessons. He thought learning something new would keep me involved with others. So, I went to Wichita State University, enrolled as a student for audit status and continue taking golf lessons.

It didn't take me long to get hooked, especially being on the golf course early in the morning. Not that I would ever be a contender, but just able to join friends for an evening on the driving range. It has been good for me.

He also asked if I played bridge as he shared his scores at the Country Club of North Carolina, CCNC. When Faye and Jim asked if I would like to join them at the Senior Center in Newton where they played bridge, I thought it would be challenging mentally to learn something new. Faye started teaching me, first at their home, then branched out to the SCN. It is fun and I try to join them when I can, expanding my circle of friends.

It was easy to have DeeDee, Faye and Jim at the ranch for dinner or overnight frequently. As friends have become fewer or are in poor health, guests at the ranch have declined. Ron is there frequently for he has a growing herd of Scottish Highland cattle that needs constant attention.

In July of 2005, things were not going well with Cleah, and her children decided it would be best if she move to assisted living near Laguna Beach where Sue and Erin could care for her. Linda would be leaving California to go back east to be with her children, so Cleah would be alone at home. By the end of the month they had packed her things, sold the house and moved her to Aegis in a lovely apartment.

In late August, Cleah had a heart attack at the center. They left her unattended too long and her dementia worsened due to oxygen deprivation. She'd been in a hospital and then moved to a skilled nursing facility. Marcia was there but would be leaving soon. Kenneth and I decided one of us should go to California to be with the family for she was in a declining situation. I went.

When they took her off most medicines, she recovered enough to go to the assisted living section of Aegis. At least she was in a lovely facility with what I hoped would be matching care.

As frequently as possible I had lunch with Phyllis at Yoder or McPherson and saw the boys when they were available.

Throughout the next months I spent as much time as possible with friends, going to concerts, theater, enjoying the ranch and family. Certainly a highlight of the summer was attending the Senior Open Golf Tournament in Hutchinson.

I had finished helping Kent with his book, never changing content, but rearranging a few words and punctuation. In gratitude for my help, he sent me a set of his submarine dolphins. I had earrings made and the pin converted to a necklace. I've worn them many times just because they became meaningful to me.

I decided in late 2006 I would really like to visit Helena Vignati and Joseph Anton in Prague, Czech Republic in 2007. I also wanted to meet Paul Vignati and his family who lived in Brno, Moravia, where Grandma Bolton was born. If I didn't go then, I wasn't sure if I'd ever make the trip.

I had been invited by Dick's cousins Shonna and Anthony to visit them and their two daughters, Louisa and Olivia in Vienna, Austria. Anthony is with the International

Atomic Energy Agency and I knew I would like visiting his work location.

May, they said, was a lovely time to see the country and they would all be available. They were right. The weather was lovely. I stayed at a Bread and Breakfast within walking distance of Helena's home. They could easily join me for coffee and we would take a bus, then the underground to tour much of the city.

Helena's sister died of leukemia many years ago, but left a son Michal. What a delight he is and speaks English well. He's now my contact with them. He had been in the states and came to the townhouse but didn't let me know in time and I was at the ranch so missed him. He went with us whenever work permitted.

We also had wonderful day trips into the countryside with Joseph telling me much of the history covering WWII and the occupation of Communist Russia. One book could not contain it all.

A four-hour drive took us outside the Bohemian territory to Brno, Moravia, where Grandma Bolton was born. There we met Paul, Maria, and their daughter Jana Vignati. He is the grandson of great-grandfather Vignati. Until our meeting he had not known a member of the family came to America.

Maria had made a wonderful Czech meal for us. It was a difficult visit for Helena for their families were separated by political and estate differences. They had not seen each other for more than 10 years.

I left Prague and went by train to Vienna where Shonna and the girls met me at the train station. We spent the weekend enjoying so much of the city and the girls were a delight. I especially enjoyed touring the International Atomic Energy Agency where Anthony is a nuclear engineer on staff.

A tour of two castles with great history, one with

Shonna, the other with the family, wonderful meals at home for Shonna is an excellent cook, and a concert with the Mozart Symphony in Mozart Hall were all treats for me.

Our day trip to the Belvedere Castle, which overlooked the lovely Austrian countryside, was filled with memories of a spectacular day.

I took the new Italian, magnetic connected, electric train back to Prague for my last three days of the trip with Helena. I wish travel were not so expensive and I could see her more frequently. She has become a very special friend as well as a relative.

Upon my return in May, plans were in full swing for the highlight of 2006, Kristen and Justin's wedding in the beautiful historic Our Lady of Sorrows, Catholic Church in Kansas City, Missouri. The crown at the alter of the church is where Mr. Hall came to pray for his new company – well known as Hallmark. It is near Hall Center and was selected by the two because it is preserved as a historic site so it would likely still be standing as long as they were.

It was a beautiful wedding as reflected in the photographs. The reception was held at the Embassy Suites with a dinner, and great dance music.

My continued service on the Alzheimer's Leadership Council kept me involved with the Memory Walk and raising money for research and day-care sponsorship. I was second highest fundraiser for the event, an achievement I'm not likely to repeat for it took a lot of time and work. How much longer I can emotionally be active with the group is a question. I have a commitment to the Carrolls that I will complete.

For more than a decade, again, I joined Kathy and Ron's family at the Lake of the Ozarks for Thanksgiving. I stayed in one of the condos in the complex to be near the family. There was no heat and any access to bedding was in the unused but locked bedroom. As I was leaving, I found the switch to the auxiliary heating system which had not been turned on during my stay. A valuable lesson.

Our time together for Christmas was brief. After our gift exchange, I wondered if my family would ever gather at my home again to celebrate. The years are changing who will be where, as grandchildren create their own traditions in their own homes. Change can come hard as the family situation changes over the years. Katie was going back to Dallas, Kristen and Justin to Kansas City and Danny to Lawrence.

More and more I find myself counting my blessings for all that I have been given. The future is open and I looked toward a new year with hope new adventures were still to come.

On Valentine's Day I was really surprised to receive a lovely bouquet of red roses with a red and white teddy bear from Kent with a note thanking me for my support saying, "You have been a Godsend during Betty's illness." That's when I became aware of Betty's declining health. His e-mail became more frequent regarding her health. Hospice had been working with them for months.

In March, I tried to give him a break by getting him involved with March Madness and the University of Kansas and playing the University of North Carolina. We had fun exchanging bets and watching the games miles apart.

It was not different than the sharing we had been doing for three years to keep each other current in our lives. He'd report his golf or bridge scores, his activities with friends, his church lunch group which included a couple from Kansas. Our e-mail contacts had become part of our lives keeping us interested, young, healthy and laughing, making me more sensitive to the reality that it takes so little to bring joy and hope into another person's life.

Then there comes a time when the Alzheimer's patient reaches the final phase and each person's closure is different, so unpredictable.

He had followed along as I did with Dick, being with Betty to help her with lunch every day. Out of devotion, if you are available, there is no way you cannot be in attendance.

About all I could say was to be prepared, for the decline can devour the body. Everything else is already gone. This will be the roughest part for you and your children, especially if they see their mother waste away. The long, lonely, painful, unspoken, spiritless, goodbye that Nancy Reagan spoke of so eloquently.

I had listened to so many in our Alzheimer's support group say the most difficult part is not being able to tell the person goodbye and have them know that you love them as much now as you did when they were alive and vital in your life. There is and has been for so very long, no response. I did my best to convey that message to Kent.

By the end of April, he was counting the days and expecting their children to arrive. There was little more I could do or say as they completed the journey with Betty. I was reminded of the stone house on the prairie legacy I had equated to Dick's departure almost four years ago.

In one of his last notes to me he said: You have been a Godsend during Betty's illness. Similar to the many times he had thanked me for being a very special friend with positive thoughts and prayers for his family. Those words of thanks, gratitude and appreciation made any effort of support on my part a blessing in my life.

During this time, I had the neighborhood garage sale and faced cattle problems at the ranch. I spent time at the ranch helping Ron with a daily cattle watch. On the last day, I almost cut my little finger off when I fell into the barbed wire fence feeding the last of the calves. I made it to the clinic to have it properly cared for and stitched back together.

In the first week of May, our longtime and dear friend Amy Feldner called to tell me Bob had died in her arms at home. They were having a memorial in Lincoln, California, and would not be coming back to Wichita. I asked her if she'd like some company. Yes, she said.

I'd planned to be in Kansas City on May 22 to go with Kristen to see the Broadway play "Wicked." So, I made arrangements to continue from there to spend a few days with Amy.

That night, Sue called to tell me they were planning to move Cleah to a Comfort Care Home where she could have better care at much less the cost than Aegis – could I come help her? Of course, I called and changed my ticket to go to Los Angeles and spend Memorial Day weekend helping them. I could spend nights with Erin and Andrew and be with Cleah during the day.

I had a wonderful afternoon and evening with Kristen and Justin, to see the Broadway show "Wicked," dinner and a tour of his office. The next day was one of rest for my plane did not leave until after five. Kristen took me to the airport after work.

On the flight from Kansas City to Sacramento, a feeling of calm relief came over me and I thought, at that moment, Betty has finally rested. I wondered which of the children had made it in to be with Kent.

I had four great days of hanging out with Amy, not doing much but going to see friends, working out at the gym, talking about great times and memories of the four us at church, walking, RVing and being great friends. It was sad but fulfilling.

Amy drove me to the airport and Andrew met me at the LAX airport, ready for another supporting role.

They were a day late getting Cleah's room ready at the new home so we had a day for some quality time with Ed, his wife, Carmeletta, and their 20-month-old daughter.

During my stay, I slept in Erin's sunroom, which has a wonderful, expansive view of the Pacific Ocean. I was not in contact with anyone on Internet and felt very separated.

At dawn I sat up to gaze at the water, I don't ever remember feeling as though distance was as great a problem. Not identified, just a vast space separating me from much of what my world had become.

There is a line from a greeting card, "The Distance Between Friends' Homes is Never Far." It seemed that way now. Space was not the only distance, time could also be included. So many years had passed filled with cherished memories.

I am in my diamond year, and completing my book project for my grandchildren. I would not have started it, let alone finished it, had it not been for Kent's encouragement. He was right, now I'm pleased to have some opportunities and limitations recorded. He will be entering his 83rd year and I hope will soon publish his book for his children. We had shared so many stories of the times and fulfilling lives we each had led. Wonderful memories.

Perhaps it was the ocean that pulled my thoughts toward Kent and all the time he spent aboard ship on it and wondering how he and the family were managing. At that final stage, Betty could not have survived many more days. I cried for them, prayed for them. In a way, those moments were also closure for me.

It was also sad but hopeful that I left Cleah in a lovely home, a comfortable room and prayed that she could adjust to the more active life and the new people. Erin, Andrew, Sue and Robert had been so very gracious to me to make the visit possible.

During my flight back from Los Angeles to Kansas City and then in the long evening drive home on the turnpike, I had a lot of time to meditate and remember. It was also a time to wonder about the future and the cries of loneliness from those around me. I knew it was time for me to distance myself from direct involvement with the problems of Alzheimer's. It weighs too heavy.

Upon arriving home I checked the computer to learn

of any news. And there it was, the feeling on the plane on Friday, May 23rd had been right. Kent had sent a message to friends of Betty's death on that day. I wept for him and his family, not so much for the loss but for the release God had finally granted.

Marge, Dick's sister, and I went to Council Grove to hear the Symphony on the Prairie. An excellent outdoor program performed by the Kansas City Symphony. Beverly and Norman Scott rode with me so I had a pleasant drive across the Flint Hills.

I had a few notes from Kent. It had been such a long goodbye and he had been so very devoted to Betty. He had a much rougher and longer time than many I've helped go through the journey with Alzheimer's.

After 50 years of friendship, even more with Dick, I hope we stay in contact. The situation is bound to change from our days with Kent and Betty, Dick and me as friends over years, exchanging family notes, promotions, travel and visiting in each other's homes.

Betty's delayed internment in Arlington National Cemetery, an honor she earned as a devoted navy wife and so richly deserved, will be held August 25. I pray the private services help bring closure and comfort to all the Carroll family.

During the past three years, I learned firsthand what Dick meant when he said of his dearest friend:

"Vice Admiral Kent Carroll is as near perfect a man as you shall ever know."

What a blessing Kent has been in my life during Dick's illness and since his passing.

I shall always cherish and return his special friendship, support and compassion.

Most of all, I thank him for restoring in me that which I promised Dick to keep – a zest for living.

Celebrating a Zest for Living

CELEBRATING MY BIRTHDAY
...at the townhouse.   ...at the ranch.

It seems ironic indeed that when I began this project, I decided to end it with my diamond year. As I have begun this celebration so many people, commitments, places and events are separating or coming together.

I volunteered many months ago to help with the fundraising event for the Alzheimer's Association at the R.C.R. Golf Tournament at Willowbend Golf Course. Little did I know how meaningful the day would become. When I made the commitment to Kent and Betty Carroll to journey with them to the end of Betty's Alzheimer's illness, I had no clue when it might end. As I worked on the golf course, it all came together. Kent is an avid golfer so I can release him to his beloved game in good health and spirits. Betty's struggle is over. What a better place or time could there be than this to say, the commitment has been fulfilled.

These pictures reflect my continuing to have a "zest for living" with friends and family whom I cherish.

With Beverly at Eastminster Presbyterian Church.

Annual birthday lunch with Kevin Nichols, broker at UBS.

DeeDee, Faye and I at Cracker Barrel.

Marge Setter and I have celebrated birthdays for more than 30 years, Theresa Cromwell joins us.

Cowtown staff recognition at 50th Anniversary, and Micha and Josiah's first visit to Cowtown where Grandmother Craig worked as a girl at the Munger House.

Dinner with Kenneth and Jane before "Les Miserables" at Music Theatre Wichita.

Closing out Junior Golf with Holly Anderson at Clapp Golf Course.

Marcia, Linda, Justin's visit (with Kenneth and Steve).

At ranch with Linda and Marcia.

Election board training.

Reunion of Sampson cousins, Ross, Kenneth, Lilly Gay and Edith.

When visiting longtime and ill KPW friend Eleanor Mayne, who first suggested I write this book, I told her of my pending trip east to include Chapel Hill, NC. She asked if I would please visit her sister Mary Ann Yakel in Pinehurst, NC on my way. She thought if I would, we would become good friends and stay in contact with each other. I promised her I would make the visit sometime in September.

Kristen and I celebrate together with Ron and Kathy at Red Rock Cafe and "Mama Mia."

Marge Hayes, Beverly Hoover, Norman Scott at Symphony on the Prairie at Council Grove, KS.

A gift from Kenneth at Jane's.

Kathy's stained glass window at the ranch.